KAIROS PREACHING
SPEAKING GOSPEL TO THE SITUATION

DAVID SCHNASA JACOBSEN
ROBERT ALLEN KELLY

Fortress Press
Minneapolis

For gospel is not the possession of the church: good news must always be discovered and rediscovered by the church—heard again in all of its newness and goodness; heard, that is to say, in relation to the specifics of the here and now. The disciple community formulates its articulation of good news only as it experiences and seeks to comprehend the bad news that is just at this moment oppressing God's beloved world.

—Douglas John Hall, *The Cross in Our Context*

KAIROS PREACHING
Speaking Gospel to the Situation

Cover image: Neutral Colored Background © Melanie Lloyd, 2009. Used under
                 license from Shutterstock.com
Cover design: Paul Boehnke

Library of Congress Cataloging-in-Publication Data
Jacobsen, David Schnasa.
   Kairos preaching : speaking Gospel to the situation / David Schnasa Jacobsen,
Robert Allen Kelly.
       p. cm.
   Includes bibliographical references and index.
   ISBN 978-0-8006-6250-9 (alk. paper)
   1. Preaching. I. Kelly, Robert Allen, 1948- II. Title.
   BV4222.J33 2009
   252—dc22

                            2009022542

The paper used in this publication meets the minimum requirements of American National Standard for Information Sciences—Permanence of Paper for Printed Library Materials, ANSI Z329.48-1984.

Manufactured in the U.S.A.

13 12 11 10 09   1 2 3 4 5 6 7 8 9 10

CONTENTS

ACKNOWLEDGMENTS

Coauthors are more aware than most that any writing is in truth a shared venture. We might imagine there are self-made authors somewhere who toil away in existential aloneness and write, in the end, not so much for an audience but for themselves. Not us. We write as those with great debts of gratitude to people far and wide. We write as those bounded by grace.

David would like to thank the Cathedral College of Preachers in Washington, D.C., for a research fellowship in November 2005. David enjoyed the gracious hospitality of Dean McDonald and all the other fine staff. During that time, the college also allowed David to sound out some of his thoughts with J. Phillip Wogaman, formerly of Wesley Theological Seminary and Foundry United Methodist Church in Washington. These people all provided a rich environment for thinking about the problem of preaching gospel in times of crisis, the material in chapter 7.

We would also be remiss if we didn't thank our seminary's confederated partner, Wilfrid Laurier University in Waterloo, Ontario. The Research Office of WLU graciously supplied a grant to hire our research assistant, Robert Nickerson, who carefully read our manuscript and otherwise helped us honor our debt to the many scholars who were our conversation partners about the gospel long before we ever started to write our little book. Of course, it didn't hurt that the grant came from our secular university partner: our seminary is trying to learn what it means to be a *public* seminary. To whatever degree our university questions, challenges, or enables us as public theologians to love the world God loves more deeply, we are grateful indeed.

Both of us are certainly grateful for our colleagues and students in theological education at Waterloo Lutheran Seminary. How many places does one get to teach, do research, preach, and worship where people, for all their differences, love to wrestle with what the gospel is and see how it creates faith and faithfulness in the world today? And get paid for it? We thank you for all that you have meant to us, and we thank you for putting up with our efforts to teach a course and write a book together.

And yet, in the end, we have to admit that we live every day bounded by the most surprising grace in our spouses, who are both careful and skillful preachers of the gospel. They had to put up with our talking, kvetching, writing, e-mailing attachments, and editing for quite some time. Its slow unfolding in classroom teaching, coffee-break discussions, and not a few revisions would try the patience of any spouse. And yet you, Nancy and Cindy, were still gracious through it all. You keep us academicians grounded in the daily and weekly work of ministry in the church and in the world.

We are grateful to all of you, named and unnamed. *Soli deo Gloria*. Let's preach the gospel!

THE SITUATIONAL SERMON AS OCCASIONAL PREACHING

There is a famous quote from one of the astronauts on the ill-fated moon shot of *Apollo 13*. You may recall that their space launch started like most of the others. For all anyone knew back then, *Apollo 13* would be as problem-free as *Apollos 11* and *12*. In fact, back in the early 1970s the whole space thing had almost grown ho-hum: "Here comes another moon landing." But it was not meant to be. Although the astronauts would not understand the breadth of the situation for some time, they could tell even as they hurtled toward the moon that there had been some kind of explosion, and now their life-support gauges were off. Later they would learn that an oxygen tank had blown. For now, though, they knew from the instrument panel that something was not right. So the astronauts radioed home. "Houston," astronaut Jim Lovell announced laconically, "we have a problem."

Those of us called to preach the gospel in today's church know the feeling all too well. We too frequently practice ministry as if we can program everything. We have our church calendars to tell us when the next big denominational emphasis is (along with all the glossy mailers from church headquarters), we have our lectionaries to help us plan the sweep of our preaching for months in advance, and we have our congregation's own rhythm: budget time in the fall, congregational meeting in the winter, and the big juridical convention in the summer. But deep down we also know that not everything can be programmed, scheduled, or planned. Paraphrasing freely Henri Nouwen, we could even say, "Ministry happens *in* the interruptions."[1] Just when we think we have it all under control and we're on our way, a beloved member of the church dies tragically or the church finances unravel or some big public issue hits us between the eyes. In moments like that, we can almost hear a plaintive voice announcing: "Church, we have a situation."

Of course, sometimes the calendars, programs, and protocols do help. Denominational resources from the national church's social justice office may just provide a way of dealing with a sticky public issue. Occasionally a lectionary text almost seems to have dropped like manna from heaven: a family dies while on vacation, and the epistle reading for the day turns out to be Romans 8:31-39. Or perhaps the juridical stewardship resources give you just the kind of focus you need to deal with that budget problem. Well, when that does happen, you're okay. You can put this book down now.

This book, however, is written for those occasions, those *situations*, when the planets don't align. It is written for those situational moments that require more than programs, lectionaries, and denominational emphases can provide. Please recall the poor souls on *Apollo 13*. Their oxygen tank problems were not written in the mission plan. There were no protocols for such situations in the various hardware manuals at Mission Control. What they needed was more than any calendar, plan, or scheduled reading could provide: they needed a word of direct address. A sweeping retelling of the narrative of American space travel from its humble advent at Kitty Hawk to its fiery Pentecost on the launchpad would be inspiring but insufficient for the situation. Reminders of scheduled mission procedures would have been irrelevant. In a situation like that, something more was called for. It was time to talk and think and act—together.

But what do you say when you really need to say something in a difficult situation? There are situations that the Bible, as central as it is to our life together as church, neither talks about nor even imagines. There are also situations that are bigger than the kinds of therapeutic insights we can offer or facilitate in the best of our pastoral care. There are also situations that cannot be merely managed according to the global economic world-view we live in between the business section in the morning paper and the closing numbers for the big stock indexes during the nightly news on TV. Could it be that situations are just the place we need something more than the conventional wisdoms of therapy and management? For situations such as these, the most helpful thing is a gospel word born of theological insight.

Of course, good week-by-week lectionary preaching also requires solid theological insight.[2] Theology is not just an "add-on" for when we have sticky church situations. It should be part of our preaching even when we follow the recurring cycles of the lectionary. What situations do, however, is bring us to a point where a "text" or a season is no longer foregrounded. Now the "situation" is the focus.

Even then, it's far too easy, when pressing situations emerge, to forget what the gospel is and to neglect theological reflection. Pragmatism runs deep in our culture. So when a death happens, we can get caught up too easily in the language of therapy and forget our theological task of proclaiming the gospel in the face of death. Or when a financial issue surfaces, we are tempted to turn a timely stewardship sermon into something that sounds like an infomercial for our ecclesiastical programs. Worse yet, a public crisis like 9/11 happens and we find ourselves so tongue-tied we have nothing gospel to say at all. It may be that in the face of such difficulties we revert to kind of prereflective "default theology," pietistic platitudes, or, worst of all, no theology whatsoever.

The Starting Point: The Good News of Justification by Grace Alone through Faith Alone

The key for preachers is to become more theologically focused on what the gospel is. The "gospel" is sometimes a term bandied about without ever being defined. It can easily become a kind of empty "cipher." For one's hearers, too often the term is confused with the final lection that is read according to the ecumenical order of the lectionary (as in, "The Gospel according to Luke"). Our goal here is to help you understand the gospel that you preach theologically. The gospel is something we as preachers can talk about, reflect on, and develop in our proclamation. It is, we contend, an incredible help for focusing one's work theologically so the preacher can know what to say in the pulpit when difficult situations emerge in parish life.

In some ways the gospel does have a discernible content and form. Some have argued that there is a kind of grammar to the gospel.[3] If so, then maybe many of us often seem to need remedial grammar lessons. For instance, in preaching, does the use of phrases like "we should," "we ought," "we must," or even "therefore let us" really allow us to speak the gospel clearly? And as for form, if our gestures and body language are marked by anxious glares or overweening finger-wagging, are we not at least at cross purposes with the gospel we want to proclaim? Surely we can perceive on one level at least that there is something of a meaning and shape to gospel proclamation.

It would be a big mistake, however, to assume that the gospel is a kind of timeless essence standing apart from life as lived.[4] It is not sufficient to identify the gospel with certain formulae ready to hand: the kerygma, Christ, Christ and him crucified, and so forth. The gospel is not like condensed soup, which only needs a couple cans of water to make reasonably palatable. No, when we talk about the gospel in *situations*, different elements of the gospel come to the fore and require our attention. For example, in Luther's day, the renewal of the proclamation of the gospel happened against the backdrop of the church's sale of papal indulgences for release from purgatory. In the process, that gospel of justification by grace through faith took a certain content and shape in connection with those contextual features (grace and works, law and gospel, etc.). A clear sense of the gospel today could not easily be reduced to a single doctrine. Yet "justification" as a *starting point* for gospel reflection could help in facing things like the tendency of global capitalism to commodify everything and everybody or the pervasiveness of the "pull-yourself-up-by-your-bootstraps" culture of success in North America. These are the kinds of gospel issues and situational tensions we explore in this book.

So in the following pages we will really be talking about a theology of the gospel. We will need to pay attention to enduring features of our common life that color our perceptions and how we "hear" and "mishear" the gospel. We will also need to understand the many varieties of occasions in ministry that will call forth some gospel word, from funeral homilies to stewardship sermons. All this is to say that preaching the gospel for such occasions when lectionaries and calendars do not help is both an exciting and demanding theological task.

The Goal: Providing Theological Helps for Situational Sermons Called "Gospel Commonplaces"

In the chapters that follow, we are not interested in promoting in the pulpit those five-dollar words and fifty-dollar phrases we all learned in our seminary systematics class: terms like hypostatic union, the ransom theory of the atonement, or *perichoresis*. Rather, we assert that the problem with thinking theologically about situations in the pulpit reflects the lack of a suitable homiletical model for doing so. If as some say, theology is "metaphorical," we can begin by exploring ways that good theology can be told in story, image, and metaphor.[5] Concrete language for theology in the pulpit could be most useful indeed.[6] Here we will show you such theology in oral units of thought we'll call gospel commonplaces.

It's probably easier to demonstrate the need for our gospel commonplaces by showing you the wealth of materials available for its more frequent counterpart in mainline Protestant and Roman Catholic preaching: the lectionary-based sermon. Let's say you decide to start with the lectionary text for the day. In that case, you have available to you for sermon preparation all sorts of resources: commentaries, lectionary helps, worship planning materials, guides to biblical preaching, Internet sermon preparation sites, and so forth. You may not always be able to access the latest scholarship on your text, but you have resources available to you that use biblical scholarship to give you some helpful ideas of what to say. In a commentary you may find a key insight or piece of background material. In a lectionary help, you might come across a beautiful illustration. On some preaching Web site, you stumble across an image that, though you need to tweak it a bit, really illumines what you want to say. These resources don't just give you information; at their best they give you means for developing what it is you actually need to say on a given Sunday in the lectionary calendar.

How different the task is if you want to speak about a problematic situation from the pulpit! You could consult the latest theological texts, but they are rarely accessible to preachers, let alone the average congregation. You might peruse the articles in theological journals, but they, too, can be quite technical. Even preaching books on theology tend to be more in the genre of "theologies of preaching."[7] While pastors should read and take advantage of such materials, there is really little that is analogous to all the preaching helps available to those who use the lectionary text rather than the situation as their starting point for preaching on a given day.

This book seeks to remedy that situation by appealing at the end of each situational chapter to gospel "commonplaces," a series of theological "topics" on which preachers can draw for developing and organizing what they want to say.

Commonplaces in Rhetoric and Theology

The idea of "commonplaces" or common topics is an old one. The term appeared first in rhetorical manuals in the ancient world. When a speaker wished to figure out what to say, he or she could use either "special topics" unique to the matter being discussed (for instance, an argument about whether to go to war against Troy would presumably include matters such as numbers of ships to get there; the costs of large, empty wooden horses; what one hoped to gain by going to war; etc.). At other points, a speaker might also use "common topics" or commonplaces, that is, arguments to which one could appeal in different kinds of speeches (such as, "from the lesser to the greater," as in, "If our troops could make short order of the mighty Minoans, how much more could they truly rout those pathetic Trojans!"). Here commonplaces refer to arguments that you could use in more than one kind of speech.[8] Given the fact that the situations of ministry are so varied, it might be helpful indeed to refer to a series of homiletical-theological "commonplaces" that one could use to put together what to say in such moments.

The idea of "commonplaces" is not just a rhetorical one, however. In fact, for a long time the Latin form of the term, *loci communes*, was used to designate theological treatises. The title was a very common one, for example, in the Reformation. Theologians like the Reformer Philipp Melanchthon wrote his famous work *Loci Communes* to make a brief compendium of Reformation theology more accessible.[9] In such a time of rapid change, books in the form of *Loci Communes* helped give early shape to emerging Protestant perspectives. In these books the "commonplaces" were the loci of theology: God, Christ, the Holy Spirit, sin, salvation, eschatology, and so forth. It treated theology as a series of "common topics" or commonplaces to reflect on the Christian faith.

Gospel Commonplaces as Theological Sermon-Helps in Ministry Situations

Our goal in this book is to give you gospel commonplaces that will aid you in your work of articulating the gospel in different situations of ministry and church life in the world. Because situations are so diverse, you'll probably need to add to or otherwise modify what we have here. A book cannot anticipate the special topics or nuances of every situation in ministry! However, it can at least give you some topics, gospel commonplaces, that will get you started. Along the way, we'll also try to develop them in ways that are more amenable to the oral task that is preaching. To do homiletical theology here means not so much to develop a peculiar language of a systematician, but to do theology in a rhetorical mode using image, story, and metaphor: that is, doing theology with hearers in mind. By providing you with gospel commonplaces, we hope to give you some basic materials to help you do your own homiletical theological work.

As heavy as that may sound, remember this: as a pastor, *you* are a resident theologian in your congregation. There are probably other people in or outside your parish who can offer better therapy to clients than you can. There are probably also other people who can manage a business better than you can. There are in the average community, however, few people who can relate with insight the unique situation of the people you know and love to the theological riches of the gospel. We hope our gospel commonplaces will help get you started. When difficult or even recurring situations pop up, you'll at least have somewhere to begin.

Our goal, then, is to identify a cluster of theological issues for gospel preachers to think about as they prepare to put their sermons together when certain "situations" arise. Our commonplaces, our homiletical *loci communes*, will not be exhaustive. We will endeavor, however, to make them accessible. Even if you don't choose to use one or more of them in your situational sermon, we hope that they will inspire you (1) to do your own theological work and (2) get your own theological imagination into high gear so you can proclaim the gospel word right where you are.

A Preview: Gospel, Context, and Situation

As we get started, it is important to note that we are using the terms *gospel*, *context*, and *situation* in a particular way. Part of the reason for this is historical. For the last five years we have cotaught a course on the topic of situational preaching to senior students at Waterloo Lutheran Seminary. While we hope to help our students integrate what they learn in preaching class with what they learn in systematic theology class, our overarching goal is a senior student who is able to be a "reflective practitioner" himself or herself. In other words, we want above all to place the tools of good homiletical and theological reflection into the hands of those about to be ordained so that they can do the difficult and demanding theological work that is serving as a pastor to a congregation.

In order to do this, we have needed to distinguish between three features in congregational life that can only be separated out with some difficulty. The first is the *gospel* we described above: the message of good news that shapes preaching in terms of its form, content, and purpose. The second is *context*, which we are calling the enduring social, cultural, and political features that color the ways in which we who live in the North American context hear the gospel. The third is *situation*, which for us is a moment or crisis that evokes a sense of limit/finitude or calls forth a decision.[10] The reason why it is difficult to distinguish between gospel, context, and situation is that in practice all of these elements interact. As we will demonstrate in the following chapters, it is hard to talk about gospel without considering it in context and in light of a situation.[11] What is more, the clarity with which we consider either gospel or context will be greatly enhanced as we move with specificity toward particular situations in ministry. Nonetheless, for the sake of clarity we will try to separate out gospel, context, and situation.

In the process of reading these beginning chapters, you will clearly see that the theology of the gospel articulated here is influenced by the Lutheran tradition. In one sense, it is quite natural to be so particular. Although David is United Methodist and Bob is Lutheran, both of us have been teaching for many years at a Lutheran seminary. Our dialogue about these matters proceeds quite naturally out of that predominantly Lutheran academic context. Nonetheless, pastors of other denominations need not fret that an adapted Lutheran theology of the gospel is utterly irrelevant to their realities. Protestants and Roman Catholics alike share a commitment to preaching the gospel.[12] After all, the gospel of God's free gift of grace is hardly under Lutheran copyright.[13] Even if some sort of adaptation is required of the reader because of the variety of theological traditions today, such adaptation is certainly of a piece with this whole book. Our gospel commonplaces will be *starting points* for you and your situational preaching ministry. We trust there will be something of value for you whether you are Lutheran, United Methodist, Presbyterian/ Reformed, Baptist, UCC, Disciples, Episcopal/Anglican, or Roman Catholic. As with any situational enterprise, you will need to engage the issues in your way in your own unique situation.

For each of our chapters on situations of parish ministry, we will follow a clear outline. At the beginning of each situational chapter, we will consider matters of context. What are the enduring features of life socially, culturally, politically, and economically that impinge on this moment for proclamation? After that, we will attend to the situation itself. Here we will try to articulate the varieties of ways these situations present themselves. As a result of reflecting on context and situation, we'll offer some practical implications for preaching in those moments. In other words, wrestling with the gospel in light of one's context and situation will give the preacher pause to think about what he or she wants to *emphasize* and *avoid* saying from the pulpit in those times. Finally, each chapter will close with a list of gospel commonplaces. These are the homiletical payoff for situational preachers. Since there are several commonplaces for each situational sermon type, preachers can simply choose one commonplace as a theme for the whole situational sermon, or use more than one if it helps them to string together an unfolding gospel reflection that moves through a series of thoughts to a new understanding or insight. In this way we bring together practical resources that represent the best of both contemporary homiletics and systematic theology.

In order to see the project through, however, we will need to use our understandings of the gospel in context in more than just abstract situations. So after this introduction, where we treat gospel, context, and situation in more general terms, we will next turn to consider certain types of situations that parish pastors face. Chapters 3 and 4 deal with the most prominent and recurrent of these situations: funerals and weddings. Although the biblical texts prescribed by denominational books of worship for funerals and weddings are useful, they often do not help the preacher to reflect more directly on the theological meaning of the specific situations before them. These two chapters will offer gospel commonplaces to help pastors "think through" what they need to say theologically in such situations. While the therapeutic arts of good pastoral care are indispensable to both funerals and weddings and the many acts of ministry that surround them, there are also theological tasks in these situations and they need to be grounded in something more than mere therapeutic insight or culturally defined common sense for living. The question we will ask here is: What is the gospel we preach in the face of death and on the threshold of shared life together? Most preachers will know these situations intimately. We hope they will enjoy reflecting on them theologically with us in light of the gospel we are all called to preach.

With chapters 5, 6, and 7, we turn to other situations that recur in contemporary parish life, but that are in all likelihood less common than funerals and weddings. Chapter 5 considers "Preaching Gospel and Stewardship." While many preachers will discuss stewardship in their week-to-week lectionary-based sermons, there are situations in parish life that call for preachers and congregations to reflect more directly on matters before them. For some it may be a looming budget crisis; for others it may be an annual stewardship drive; for still others it could result from a new direction in ministry. Whatever the particulars of the situation, it will be useful to remember that stewardship sermons are not just barely baptized fund-raising appeals. They can be occasions for preaching the gospel. We will consider in chapter 5 some gospel commonplaces that could be useful in many kinds of sermons for situations calling for stewardship.

Chapter 6 looks at "Preaching Gospel in the Face of Injustice." Again, regular lectionary preaching offers many opportunities to talk about justice in the pulpit. Many texts will also lend themselves to be applied in passing to various situations of importance to congregations. However, no text or lectionary possesses infinite hermeneutical elasticity. Moreover, situations of injustice do present themselves to congregations in the world. Such situations may just call for more direct gospel speech. With chapter 6 we hope to offer gospel commonplaces to preachers who are confronted with a situation of injustice.

Chapter 7 then turns to moments that are indeed occasional but typically hold the awareness of people in the pew like no other: times of public crises. On Sundays such as those after the space shuttle *Columbia* disaster, the Asian tsunami, the declaration of war in Iraq, or 9/11, what do you say? Clearly chapter 7 cannot fill in the blanks for all moments like these, since they are by nature so different. However, we can outline some gospel commonplaces that will get you started. Many authors and commentators observed that church attendance was up briefly after 9/11. Instead of lamenting that those people did not stay, perhaps we could ask what we *should* say. How do we speak the gospel in the shadow of such awful events? This is precisely the place where preaching and theology can serve God's people in the world.

In our brief final chapter, we invite you to join in the act of theological reflection for preaching. Here the situation is the recurring one of out-church public preaching. It could be the result of an invitation to speak at a baccalaureate, or a Veterans Day event, or on an issue at a denominational meeting at a juridical level. We chose this chapter because such moments outside of congregational meeting do recur. More importantly, however, it gave us a chance to develop a way of inviting you more closely into the process. You can, therefore, by the end of this book anticipate your own "graduation." We hope to help you claim your vocation as a residential theologian of the gospel.

"Church, We've Got a Situation . . . *and* a Gospel to Preach"

We suspect that the situations we are considering are more than familiar to you. We hope that you'll enter this process as we have: in the spirit of conversation. As professors in our class at Waterloo Lutheran Seminary, we point out to our students at the beginning of the semester that the two of us sometimes disagree. While that sometimes throws the keeners in class who try to figure out whom to suck up to in order to get a good grade, for most people our confession of occasional disagreement actually opens a door. We will not all consider the gospel we preach, the contexts in which it is preached, and the situations we face in the same way. In fact, there's a good chance that the situations that confront us will have their own unique features and shape where we are. We hope our conversation with you here will be a door to a way of thinking about ministry using tools of both homiletics and systematics. We're not asking that you agree with us as much as we are asking you to reflect as a homiletical theologian in your own time and place.

With that, however, we should still confess one thing we hold in common with each other and with you, the reader. What we as preachers do have is a sense that we are called. At some point someone has laid or will likely lay hands on us and say: "Go, preach the gospel." While on most Sundays we will find joy in doing so in light of prescribed readings and the rhythms of calendars, there will be Sundays and other days when a situation will interrupt the normal flow. We want to help you think about your call to preach the gospel on days like that—on days when we must say: "Church, we've got a situation here."

CHAPTER 1

THEOLOGY OF THE GOSPEL

In those rare moments when lectionaries and pericopes don't offer hermeneutical paths to thinking about situations that emerge in parish life, where do preachers of the gospel start? We startß by thinking theologically about the gospel message. The next question, then, is, What is the gospel? Don't worry too much: the question of the gospel was as complex for our diverse biblical writers as it is for us. Take, for example, the opening of the Gospel of Mark: "The beginning of the good news of Jesus Christ, the Son of God" (Mark 1:1). And yet a few verses later Mark continues: "Jesus came to Galilee, proclaiming the good news of God, and saying, 'The time is fulfilled and the kingdom of God has come near; repent, and believe in the good news'" (vv. 14-15). Within a scant fifteen verses, Mark himself defines gospel "good news" in two ways: the gospel is "Jesus Christ, the Son of God" and yet also the message of the coming of God's kingdom! The gospel for Mark, therefore, is indeed about Christ and yet, together with Christ, points beyond Christ himself to God and the fulfillment of God's kingdom in this "time." Notice that even with Mark the gospel doesn't give us a simple content (the "kerygma," some atonement theory, or any other simple formula) but does invite us to think through a structure of thought (Christ, and yet Christ's pointing toward the kingdom) toward God's intentions for the world at this time.

We live in a culture that values pat formulae of problem and solution. Watch a typical television commercial and you see it clearly. There is a *serious* problem, such as "ring around the collar" that is caused by some sinner using Brand X. This problem threatens the peace and security of both the sinner and the sinner's victim. A Voice from Above (often in the form of a nosy neighbor) reveals the solution: the transcendent truth of New, Improved Whatever. The solution is applied, and the former sinner and her target are transported to paradise (often Las Vegas or Hawaii).[1] Because this plot has proven so useful to advertisers, we preachers are tempted to use it, too. Our sermons can become overly long commercials for the new, improved Jesus, or for ourselves.

Preaching the gospel in the situations of life, community, and world is a bit more complex than the plot of a commercial. The gospel is not a problem/solution plotline. Because the gospel is God's *promise*, it can never be the guarantee of a solution, nor can preaching tried and true formulae guarantee that the gospel will be communicated in the present. A promise from God always invites us into faithful hope that requires theological reflection. Because the gospel is a promise and not a guarantee, it leads us toward a way of thinking through situations, an unfolding of the meaning of hope and trust in God's promise in Christ. That is why in what follows we will present *loci communes*, gospel commonplaces, which are signposts pointing to where the trail begins rather than static formulae that deny that walking the trail is necessary.[2] What you find in these pages does not give you the one, single, universally applicable solution to some problem. Instead, we invite you to join us in a reflective process. We see our role as helping you do your own work as a theologian of the gospel. While we cannot determine the "answer" or "solution" or the best way to communicate the gospel for you where you are, we can invite you into a process of theological reflection that enables you to structure your own thought, drawing on gospel commonplaces with a view toward your own situation. The question here in this chapter is not, What is the answer?—we'll leave that to the ad whizzes on Madison Avenue. Rather, the question here is, How do we start?

Justification by Grace through Faith as Gospel Starting Point

Our starting point for thinking through the gospel situationally will be the doctrine of justification by grace through faith. While we have made the case in the introduction why this starting point might be useful for people from various theological traditions, we have not said anything about *how* this could be so. We see this starting point as being useful for both hermeneutical and heuristic reasons.

Hermeneutically the doctrine is significant because of its role in Christian interpretation of the Bible. Although the New Testament writers are not of one mind about the doctrine, there is a sense in which the doctrine is central to early Christian articulation of its gospel message. Thus, while Luke's understanding of justification in the parable of the Pharisee and tax collector (Luke 18:9-14) sounds little like Paul's elaborated views in Romans 3 and 4, the New Testament as a whole does seem at least to wrestle with justification and questions of righteousness. Biblical scholar John Reumann goes so far as to say that righteousness/justification represents a central theme of the Bible as a whole.[3] Its centrality, therefore, gives us some useful guidance in thinking through our theological task. The claim we would make, the claim of the Lutheran movement, is that justification by grace though faith is the central hermeneutical lens through which we interpret the diversity of Scripture. This represents a starting point for theology that is, we believe, in continuity with the gospel proclamations to which the Scriptures themselves bear witness.

This brings us to our second reason for using justification by grace through faith as our starting point for situational gospel reflection: its usefulness as a heuristic tool. The word *heuristic* goes back to a Greek verb that means "to find" (*heuriskein*) and is defined by *Webster's Dictionary* as "helping to discover or learn."[4] The idea is that our gospel starting point of justification by grace through faith helps us to discover or learn something about situations that launches us off into further exploration and theological reflection. In a sense, this heuristic use is not all that different from how some have described justification by grace through faith, namely, as a critical principle for doing theology. While the doctrine of justification of faith is not the "solution" to situational problems, it helps heuristically to shake things loose. While the gospel commonplaces will represent different loci or commonplaces of theology, this "core" doctrine will make room for us to "explore" a new gospel horizon for the kinds of situations we face.

Critical Presuppositions Going Forward

If we are to use this doctrine as our starting point for the work that follows, we also need to acknowledge some of the presuppositions that shape our use of this starting point. Three of the presuppositions arise because of the doctrine of justification itself, while one of them represents a problem with the doctrine as it has often been understood.

One presupposition is that the doctrine of justification offers a word of radical grace in any context and situation. The gospel is God's unconditional promise for the future of creation made in the resurrection of the crucified Jesus. Given the moralism that predominates in our culture, whether in advertisements and public media or even pious conceptions of the religious life and its relation to certain moral values, the doctrine of justification sounds an unequivocal word of gospel grace. Our observation is that much of the wider culture operates on a different calculus than unconditional promise.[5] Given our context, therefore, this doctrine is uniquely suited for proclaiming a gospel of radical grace in a context where we cannot depend on the word of God's promise being already present.

This leads to a second presupposition, and one of exceeding importance for us: the notion that the word of the gospel is itself *extra nos*, that is, "outside of us." The importance of this idea is that it helps us to articulate a gospel that is theocentric, or God centered, rather than anthropocentric, or human centered. For the gospel to be good news, it needs to disclose not what we human beings do or need to do, but rather what *God* is doing to redeem. The good news is the gospel of God in Christ, not the gospel of what we need to do to get our lives together. While God does use human and earthly things to speak this *extra nos* gospel word to us (e.g., the voices of preachers, the words of Scripture, the waters of baptism, and the bread and wine of the Eucharist), God's gospel word is not resident in the psyches of preachers and celebrants or hearers, but remains God's own living voice. Incarnation is God's own way to move toward us with the gospel: God comes to us in the flesh. God joins Godself to our little preaching words and to sacramental elements precisely because God is God. Whether the incarnate Christ or in word and sacrament, though, God is still other. This *extra nos* of the word reminds us that the gospel is both from God and about God, neither from us nor about us. It aids us in proclaiming a gospel in which the word becomes flesh.

A third presupposition of this work is that justification by grace through faith is a matter of divine promise[6] and always has an eschatological shape. To say that the gospel is God's promise is to make several claims. The most basic is that the promise is God's and is therefore unconditional in a way that human promises never can be. The same God who created the universe *ex nihilo* also promises to bring all creation to completion in spite of our efforts to abort the project before its time. When God raised the crucified Jesus from the dead, God promised once and for all that the destiny of creation is good. Despite us, God's promise will prevail in the end.

To claim that the gospel is promise is to claim that the gospel is *a* promise and not a guarantee. This means that the appropriate response is hope and trust. A promise, even an unconditional promise, also contains within itself an ambiguity. God is most certainly faithful and trustworthy, but we know that on the basis of faith, not sight. What has been promised has not yet been revealed in its fulfillment, and even when the fulfillment comes, promise and fulfillment are not connected in the way that cause and effect are. What we are promised is a justified destiny, but what we are now is *simul iustus et peccator*, simultaneously saints and sinners. What we are promised is the reign of God, but what we see now is the rule of humanly devised institutions. What we are promised is a renewed creation, but what we see is a world in desperate need of renewal. What we are promised is the Savior of the *cosmos*, but what we see is the crucified Jesus.

By articulating the gospel as promise, we preserve the quality of faith as well as radical grace. Justification by grace *through faith* reminds us of the "already but not yet," proleptic character of the gospel promise. Especially in the earlier part of his career, Luther often pointed to the statement in Hebrews that "Faith is the assurance of things hoped for, the conviction of things not seen" (Heb. 11:1).[7] The goal of gospel-shaped situational preaching is not to make once and for all pronouncements about the contingent world we live in as if everything were all "settled" and life now unambiguous, but to speak the promises of God in the midst of the ambiguous and sometimes even mysterious realities we face. Gospel speech is grounded in present reality while refusing to consign to a fixed past what actually participates in an open and still unknown future. Thus, it articulates hope-filled faith in the midst of suffering and life.

The fourth and final presupposition is an enlargement of some pietistic and individualistic conceptions of the *pro me* ("for me") of the gospel. In these readings the *pro me* of the gospel has too often been understood to exclude the world God loves and human social life in the name of a penal substitution that is perceived in largely individualistic terms. We find Dietrich Bonhoeffer's emphasis on the *pro nobis* ("for us") and *pro aliis* ("for others") character of the doctrine of justification to be more helpful. Insofar as societal, political, and cultural forces participate in strategies of self-justification, the doctrine of justification by grace through faith by its very nature speaks to broader social realities than just the tortured individual conscience.[8] The world of creation—the *cosmos*—and the world of

social and political life—the *polis*—belong to God as much as
the interior *psyche* of the troubled conscience belongs to God.
God is gracious to sinners, and it seems hard to claim that God
would be somehow less gracious to *cosmos* and *polis* than to
psyche.[9]

A Lutheran Theology of the Gospel in Postmodern Context

From its very beginning, the Lutheran theological movement
has been about a theology of the gospel and has had a central
understanding of what that gospel is. Philipp Melanchthon's
words in the Augsburg Confession both set and sum up that
tradition:

> Furthermore, it is taught that we cannot obtain forgiveness
> of sin and righteousness before God through our merit,
> work, or satisfactions, but that we receive forgiveness of sin
> and become righteous before God out of grace for Christ's
> sake through faith when we believe that Christ has suf-
> fered for us and that for his sake our sin is forgiven and
> righteousness and eternal life are given to us. For God will
> regard and reckon this faith as righteousness in his sight as
> St. Paul says in Romans 3 and 4.[10]

We might well ask here Luther's catechetical question, "What
does this mean?" Especially in an age when concepts like "for-
giveness of sin" and "righteousness before God" are foreign to
most ears, and what "faith" and "grace" mean to most people
is nothing like what Luther and Melanchthon meant by those
words, we need to be clear about what theology of the gospel
we are confessing.

Most Lutheran theologians of the last generation or two
have been generally agreed that the gospel is God's word of
unconditional promise spoken in Christ and in the preaching
of the church. In the words of Eric Gritsch and Robert Jenson,
"According to the Reformation insight and discovery, the gospel
is a wholly unconditional promise of the human fulfillment of its
hearers, made by the narrative of Jesus' death and resurrection.

The gospel, rightly spoken, involves no ifs, ands, buts, or maybes of any sort. . . . The gospel says, 'Because the Crucified lives as Lord, your destiny is good.'"[11] Gritsch and Jenson here express the core of the mainstream North American Lutheran view of the meaning of the doctrine of justification, a consensus that formed the way the two of us learned the doctrine and the way we teach it. At the center of the gospel is radical grace, the radically unconditional promise that God makes to creation in Christ.

The gospel expressed in this way, at least among Lutherans, has two corollaries. The first is that talk about the gospel is always talk about the crucifixion of Jesus of Nazareth. In the twentieth century this insight was made forcefully in Walther von Loewenich's *Luther's Theology of the Cross* and in a series of systematic studies that followed from von Loewenich's insights.[12] The most important of these insights is that the crucifixion of Jesus is not just one point of a doctrine of the atonement, but is the paradigmatic event of Christian theology as a whole. Everything the church says and does is refracted through the cross. The second, and very much related, corollary is the "eschatological reservation." This is the insight that Christian life in this world here and now is lived with the full consciousness of the resurrection of the crucified Jesus and in the full consciousness that the reign of God has not yet come in its fullness. The cross continues to be both a promise and a shadow. Christians are *simul iustus et peccator*, simultaneously justified saints and sinners under judgment. The risen Christ still carries the wounds of crucifixion on his body. These intertwined themes will in some way be part of speaking the gospel. In many of the *loci* in the following chapters the observant reader will notice that no matter where we go, we typically end up with the meaning of the crucifixion of Jesus for whichever theme we are pursuing at the moment.

If this contemporary understanding of the doctrine of justification has any weakness, it is that it most often has a more individual focus rather than communal focus in the way that it is taught. At a time when many see the problems of hyper-individualistic consumerism, we must ask how to express the doctrine of justification so that it is not heard as a religious affirmation of the therapized consumer cocooned in a giant SUV. Is it time for a little "narrative chaos"? What story are we telling when we tell the story of the sinner forgiven by grace? Are we telling the story of what God has done in the resurrection of the crucified Jesus, or are we telling some other story?

An Excursus: Expressing the Gospel of Grace in the Postmodern Context

Let us illustrate what we mean with a little excursus into how we might express the gospel for a postmodern audience. What follows is a bit of an experiment that should help the reader see what we mean when we say that there are multiple ways to express the doctrine of justification by grace alone through faith alone in our current context.

One of the issues placed before us by the postmodern and deconstructionist philosophers such as Jacques Derrida and Emanuel Levínas is the reality of the other. Otherness or "alterity" has become central to philosophical and literary discussion, and works on the topic seem to be popping up in all directions and in all disciplines. What the philosophers have reminded us is that the one who is other than ourselves has a crucial claim on our attention. We have, in modernity, tended to see ourselves as subject and the other as object and we have come to believe that we can be objective in our study of and relation to the other. The postmodernists challenge the claim to objectivity and deny the distinction between subject and object as a glossing over of the chasm between self and other. Some even challenge the existence of something known as a "self" as a delusion. This is all contested territory, of course, but these challenges to the intellectual worldview that provide the context for modern versions of the doctrine of justification (not to mention theology as a whole) do call upon the preacher to think carefully about how to speak the gospel so that it can be heard in the present.[13]

Otherness should not really be a strange concept to pastors. Many of us were introduced to Karl Barth in seminary and are aware that he used otherness as a central way to understand God in relationship to humanity. For Barth God is utterly transcendent, wholly other. The chasm between self and other is, in the case of God and ourselves, so deep that one begins to wonder how it can possibly be bridged, even from God's side. Contemporary theologians who have followed Barth speak of the incommensurability of gospel speaking and any other language. Whether one follows postmodernism or Barth, there is the possibility that the gulf between "self" and "other" is too deep and wide to cross.

We can see the practical evidence for this view of things in the current state of relations between Euro-American societies and Asian and African societies that are deeply influenced by Islam. For many people in our society today, the Muslim is the ultimate "other," often portrayed as the "monster" who cannot be understood, but only fought against in some ultimate apocalyptic struggle as Beowulf fought Grendel or St. George battled the dragon. We hear the expression of this kind of thinking from politicians and newscasters, pundits and (sad to say) preachers. There are also those within Islam who think much the same way about us. God or Satan, ultimate good or ultimate evil, are the only options presented. The question that animates many postmodern philosophers is how to develop a way to deal realistically with difference without resorting to the sort of apocalyptic violence that the popular view of otherness seems to entail.

If our identity and our place before God is decided already by God's unconditional promise in Christ, then our encounter with the other does not have to be objectified nor does it have to unfold in violence; there is another way. In the first place, the doctrine of justification claims that God, the Ultimate Other, encounters us not as monsters to be destroyed, but as children to be embraced. The encounter with God is not simple or easy—the doctrine of justification has never said that—but its outcome is decided by unconditional promise, not by anything else, and especially not by our own achievements or power.

Our encounter with God is not simple, because we perceive God in a variety of ways. In many situations we even perceive God as malevolent presence, as the monstrous other. Luther called this perception *Anfechtungen*, "terrors of the soul,"[14] and Søren Kierkegaard called it anxiety. We feel that God is set to destroy us, to cast us into hell itself. The only way out seems to be either to submit to destruction or to go to war against God. God as Wholly Other is God as the final source of terror. Encounter with God means death, eternal death and oblivion, and so atheism seems the only possibility if one wants to live.

But atheism is not the only possibility. As we descend into the depths of divine violence and destruction, God speaks a word to us. That word is promise: "There is hope that the impossible is possible."[15] That hope of the possible impossible is the gospel word of grace. The gospel proclaims that the God who is other than us is not out to destroy and slay, but to love and heal. The gospel word opens up the possible that is impossible, proclaims that though God is hidden and other, God is also revealed in Jesus as in the flesh and making all things new. Our sense of God as the author of monstrous violence is something from inside our own fears of what God might be (and fears that we project onto the other in many settings) and contradicts the God who is revealed in Jesus of Nazareth.

According to the gospel, even our relationships with human others are opened to new possibilities not otherwise conceivable. One way to read Luther's basic message in the Reformation is, "By the grace of God in Christ you have been set free from worrying about your own salvation; now you are free to worry about the welfare of your community." That is, since the word of God proclaims our personal salvation by grace through faith, I no longer have to spend any energy at all in the effort to secure my own individual, personal salvation. I am released from the prison that I create when my own destiny is my ultimate concern. In being honest about what really goes on inside myself, I no longer need to project the monstrous onto the other. "I" is free to be "we," and this particular "we" does not need a "them" to find its identity. Identity is a gift, not something to be secured.

The other—who also exists before God by grace alone—is free to be other, and thereby the impossible possibility of dialogue with the other is open.

This is just one way, we believe, that the gospel can be expressed in the present sociocultural situation. The gospel of unconditional promise does not just speak to the problem of the guilt I feel for the individual sins I have committed. It is not just a religious form of personal therapy. It is not even addressed only to the problem of existential estrangement and alienation. God's unconditional promise made to creation in the resurrection of the crucified Jesus speaks to anything and everything in the cosmos that is the result of the rift between Creator and creature narrated in Genesis 3. The word of promise breaks into the created world from outside, crucifying the old and creating the new, the impossible possibility, in Christ.

Gospel as Radical Promise

The proclamation of a promise that radical is the focus of preaching. As preachers our task is to preach sermons that are as radical as God's promise so that people can hear the good news that the promise is meant for them in their situation. In order to do that we need certain "rules of grammar," if you will, that help us to speak the gospel so that it is heard as the good news. One of these "rules" is that preaching must be honest and truthful about what goes on within and among humans as well as truthful about the promise of God in Christ. Following Luther, Lutherans have made this point under the heading of "the proper distinction between law and gospel."[16] By "law" the tradition means those words from God that point out the problem with our existence as creatures who refuse to recognize who we really are. One image of the law is that of a "mirror" that shows us the truth about ourselves. These words can be commands from God, or they can be promises made with conditions attached. They can also be "look what you have done now" statements. By "gospel" the tradition means the word of God that articulates the unconditional promise of God in

Christ. This is the word that justifies, that liberates, that enables discipleship.

When we say that law and gospel must be distinguished properly, we are not saying that the Hebrew Scriptures must be separated from the New Testament (both contain both law and gospel) or anything like that. The distinction of law and gospel is not some Manichean dividing of God into two, one harsh and the other compassionate. The distinction of law and gospel is also not a distinction between Judaism and Christianity or Catholicism and Protestantism. We are also not advocating an approach to preaching that first beats people up and then says something nice to them. All of these are evidence of a fundamental misunderstanding of the proper distinction of law and gospel.

The distinction between law and gospel is a paradox, not a dualism. The word of God comes to us in this paradoxical form that is, in the end, the good news of what God is doing in the resurrection of the crucified Jesus. Paradoxically, God reconciles us to Godself by first showing us how alien we are. That paradox animates the dialectic of both biblical interpretation and preaching. The preacher must be clear about the difference between law and gospel and be clear about which word is being spoken at the moment. Distinguishing law and gospel is a theological, dialectical, and hermeneutical act in which the preacher discerns the context and the situation and discerns the word the text speaks into that situation. For us, therefore, law and gospel are aids to theological reflection and discernment.[17]

The problem with preaching that confuses law and gospel is that it fails to be truthful about us and about God. We are encouraged to see ourselves either as people who really aren't so bad after all or as people who are utterly beyond any hope of salvation. We are encouraged to see God as a celestial accountant, keeping the books on who is naughty and who is nice. If we think of ourselves as nice, we thank God for making us better. If we think of ourselves as beyond naughty, we see God as the all-consuming monster who takes delight in damning sinners to hell.

Let us state it again: the only legitimate response to such nonsense is atheism. If that were who God is, then the only response with any integrity is to slay the monster. But the problem is not with God; the problem is in us and too often projected from us into our preaching. The problem is with our inability to recognize the monstrous in ourselves and our inability to hear that the wholly unconditional promise of God in Christ is spoken to us and spoken for us nonetheless. When we confuse law and gospel, we encourage the worst in Christians and leave thoughtful people no option but atheism.

Our approach, however, is not a formulaic homiletical structure, but a theological hermeneutic that begins with the hearing of the gospel and spirals through a process of reflection, which includes reading and interpreting the foundational texts in light of historical and contextual experience. Faith begins in the hearing of the gospel, and the hearing of the gospel changes everything.[18] Faith leads us into a community and into a way of life in which we question the reality we see around us and question God. In the community of faith, such questions lead us into an encounter with the sources upon which the community is built, the Scriptures and the traditions of reading those Scriptures. We try the best we can to hear what prophets, apostles, and theologians were saying to the people whom they addressed directly, a primarily historical question. The historical question pushes us further. We are pushed to interpret what these sources say to us from the perspective of the world in which we live and the life into which faith has led us. Our world of meanings comes up against the worlds of the texts and a dialogue of question and question ensues. Note that this is a dialogue of question and *question*, not a dialogue of question and *answer*. We come to the texts with our question, but the texts do not provide answers. Rather, the texts interrogate us. Taken aback by their boldness, we reformulate our questions.[19]

In this encounter we bring to interpretation not only our questions but the context within which we exist. The context is where our questions arise, but it is also much more. Our context provides us with a worldview, an ideology, a way of seeing and understanding the world around us—our world of meanings. All of this enters into the dialogue of question and question. In order to understand what God may be saying to us in Scripture and tradition, we are pressed to understand our context better. As theologians we are at the point where two worlds collide, the world of the text and the world of the context. We move back and forth on a bridge, sometimes feeling more at home on one side and sometimes more at home on the other side.

The movement of this spiral is toward action. "Praxis" is action or practice that is informed by theory. In this sense all of Christian life is praxis, action in the world informed by a (hopefully) growing understanding of the implications of the gospel. The goal of all theological interpretation is Christian praxis. At some point the questions are set aside so that action can be taken. The action of faithful praxis is a funny sort of action. In praxis the questions we have set aside for the moment come back to the fore, but they come back in a different form, a form influenced by the action, by praxis. In the midst of praxis we hear the gospel again, perhaps in a way we have never heard it before. In that hearing old questions are reformulated and new questions arise, and so a new lap of the spiral begins.

Preaching is an important part of this spiral. For the preacher, the act of preaching is a moment of praxis; for the congregation the sermon is a snapshot of interpretation that forms part of the community's movement toward praxis. The need for situational preaching arises when one particular question has presented itself to the community and must encounter the questions of Scripture and tradition. Scripture and tradition send us together with the gospel more deeply into context and situation where questions must be lived.

CHAPTER 2

GOSPEL IN CONTEXT AND SITUATION

If the gospel is, as we say, *pro nobis*, or "for us," and kenotic, or self-emptying into the world, it is actually impossible to speak of it apart from the contexts where its character as "for us" and "self-emptying into the world" is made manifest. Although we do insist that the gospel is radical grace and *extra nos*, this does not mean that the gospel can be articulated wholly apart from the world in which we live and in those occasions through which we do theological reflection. To say that Christ becomes incarnate, in the end, is to be invited into a way of thinking that relates God's word with the world God loves so much.

In the course of this chapter we will focus on two ways in which this happens: contexts and situations. Contexts, we have stated, refer to those enduring realities of culture, society, and language that shape our understanding and orient, for good or for ill, the way in which we hear the gospel. The word *context* comes from a Latin root, "to weave together," and our hearing of the gospel and the context we are in are profoundly interwoven. By understanding context, we probe what the gospel means in this time and place more deeply. The second way we will focus on this incarnational understanding of word and world is through situations. We have stated that situations are those occasions that seem to call forth gospel speech. For us, situations are specific moments that demand our attention, typically provoking, as David Buttrick says, limit moments or decision moments.[1] In this chapter we will explore situations further with a view toward understanding their role in articulating the gospel.

Behind all of this is an important notion in Lutheran theology: the finite is capable of bearing the infinite. Although we will hold to the notions of the gospel as being an *extra nos* word of "radical grace," we can also trust that our contexts, situations, our very finitude are not merely problems, but occasions for gospel speech.

On the other hand, there is still a primacy of the gospel itself. The gospel orients us to the world God loves. For this reason, we propose to view the gospel as not just a content, but also a hermeneutical lens. This means that, as we negotiate the encounter of perspectives that happens when the word comes into the world, it is the gospel that guides us in our thinking and in our acting. While gospel, context, and situation are intimately related, it is the gospel, in the end, that brings context and situation into focus and helps us to interpret what we see around us.

The relationship among the gospel, our context, and the current situation does involve preachers in an act of theological interpretation. There is, as Hans-Georg Gadamer and Paul Ricoeur would remind us,[2] a coming together of horizons, of life-worlds, that demands an interpretive act. This is not a moment when the gospel gives the answers to questions arising from the context, but one in which the gospel questions us and our perspective. These gospel questions push us toward new understandings of both context and situation and enable us to discover a way through the thicket of the decisions they require and the limits of human existence they expose.

This connection of the gospel and our contexts and situations is part of the gospel itself. The gospel is most certainly a word that comes to us from outside ourselves, but it is precisely a word of radical grace that dwells with us, good news about a God who comes among us as one of us (incarnation), a Word of God who empties himself (kenosis) of "equality with God" (Philippians 2) to be in intimate relationship with creation and human history. The good news about the God who is revealed in the birth, life, death, and resurrection of Jesus of Nazareth is always contextual and situational.

Gospel and Context

The question then becomes how we understand this relationship. In his book *Models of Contextual Theology*, Stephen Bevans describes six different approaches to relating gospel and context: Translation, Anthropological, Praxis, Synthetic, Transcendental, and Countercultural.[3]

- *Translation* more or less presupposes that the gospel is inserted into a context, just as a seed is in the ground. The context is considered "good," and is able to bear a faithful and fruitful "translation of the gospel." Once translated, the gospel is the "kernel" hidden in the "husk" of the culture.
- The *anthropological* view holds context in even higher regard. Here the gospel is already residing in the culture and its understandings. The issue for this anthropological approach is how well we can know the context so as to draw the gospel that is already there out of it.
- The *praxis* view doesn't regard the relationship of gospel and context in the kind of spatial, static, and organic perspectives above, but instead looks upon the relationship as a process in motion. In the praxis perspective, gospel and context are a process that spirals toward *social change*. While context is viewed as generally good, it is not above suspicion. In the end, relating gospel to context is not simply a matter of content, but action.
- The *synthetic* approach views the relationship of gospel and context as one of profound connection. In fact, for the synthetic view gospel and context need to be in conversation. Neither one is complete and in fact needs "the other."
- The *transcendental* model assumes that the gospel needs a context. Contexts are viewed as good and trustworthy.

The gospel in this approach is located in subjective experience but leads to ever-wider perspectives.

- Finally, the *countercultural* view understands the gospel as reliable but in need of other cultures to be understood more completely. Although some countercultural perspectives border on being *anticultural*, it is probably safer to say that this view sees culture as at least partially problematic and resistant to the gospel. Here the context is unequal to Scripture and tradition, and the gospel they articulate.

Bevans goes on to point out that the models are not absolutely discrete. In actuality people probably operate out of two or more of these perspectives. Both of us actually join more than one approach together, depending on the way and context in which we seek to do contextual theology—and on which we put the emphasis may vary from situation to situation. Bob, for example, is partial primarily to the praxis and countercultural models. David, by contrast, views culture a bit more positively and thus gravitates more toward a combination of the praxis and synthetic models. The value of such approaches to relating gospel and context becomes apparent below.

Why are such combinations important? The gospel is not some simplistic X that we can just plug in where convenient. There is a certain specificity and particularity to the gospel that we must take seriously. At the same time, in order for the gospel to be the gospel, it must be spoken aloud, put into human language within a particular sociocultural context. These two realities, both true at the same time, must be held in tension. Neither can be lost. Yet not all of us will maintain that tension in quite the same way. A person who uses the translation model or the countercultural model might well see the gospel as having a primary referent that does not change even as the way we communicate the gospel changes. A person who holds to the transcendent or synthetic model might well believe that the idea of an unchanging referent doesn't really relate to contexts. This move makes the context more or less expendable. That does not mean that the person holding to the transcendent or synthetic models sees the gospel as some Freudian inkblot on which we can project our all-too-human hopes and dreams willy-nilly. We are pointing toward an understanding of the gospel that both *focuses* (that is, makes clear) the context and is incarnate in the context. That is, the gospel both shapes contexts and, in turn, is also shaped by them.

To use ourselves as examples, when Bob joins the countercultural and praxis models of relating gospel to context, he wishes to emphasize the way in which gospel encounters, interprets, and critiques the context, so that the context is engaged by the gospel. In this way the disciple community[4] becomes a place where a foreshadowing of the reign of God can be seen. Because David joins the synthetic and praxis models, he senses that the gospel as lens focuses on culture as a means of initiating a mutual dialogue and critique in order to move toward social change. Because culture relates back to the gospel lens, however, David would be quick to point out that the culture, when passing into gospel view, occasions the focusing of the gospel lens. While the lens of the gospel works differently in both Bob and David's pairings, there is a sense in which the relationship and the process are indispensable for the theological work that is the gospel to happen at all.

The point is to establish a priority of the gospel and yet a need for ongoing exchange and transformation with context. In the process, understanding is not some timeless a priori to be applied to life, but emerges through the give and take of contextual-theological reflection and action. As this happens, our understanding of the meaning and implications of the gospel enlarge. Paul Ricoeur calls this the "surplus of meaning."[5] Even when context is sometimes problematic (for instance, What does the "gospel" story sound like in a culture dominated by success narratives?), an engagement of gospel and culture can bring new light to what the gospel means.

For example, one can see an analogous dynamic of Ricoeur's surplus of meaning in the changing metaphors used to describe a theology of atonement. In the ancient world, where so many people either were slaves or feared becoming slaves, the idea that Christ's crucifixion was a *ransom* to buy slaves free made sense. Later, in the medieval period, where the vast distinction between a lord and a serf meant that crimes were punished commensurate with the honor of the offended party, Anselm's satisfaction theory helped make sense of atonement. Our sin against the Lord, whose honor is by definition infinite, requires an infinite sacrifice to make amends—a sacrifice no human can offer, only Christ himself. The gospel meets context in different times and places, in different epochs and cultures. The theological solutions developed are both insightful and yet have become problematic as times change. As we interpret through the gospel lens and make meaning both in and *against* such contexts, the horizon of insight into the gospel becomes ever larger and clearer. Certainly no one would want to go back to slavery or medieval vassalage merely to justify a metaphor, especially when the scope of atonement theories grows and changes as new cultural epochs emerge.[6] It is, after all, God who justifies; not us!

As a result, we preachers engage the problem of situational preaching where gospel meets context as a theological activity. While it is the gospel that sets us in motion and thus has priority, it is a gospel "for us" that "pours itself out for the world." In the process, the gospel puts into human language in this time and place God's word for this now. God enters into the world in words, in water and in bread and wine and speaks the gospel as good news specifically for us. The gospel is not a word about being whisked away into another world. The gospel does what Christ does—it comes into the world God loves so much in risky, self-effacing, redemptive love. Scripture itself helps us on these points. In the famous kenotic hymn of Philippians 2, Christ does not hold to "equality with God" obsessively, but yields up "the form of God," considering "equality with God" something not to be grasped, but yielded for the other. The hymn tells the story of a costly spending of self for the world. Christologically the theme continues, at least in Pauline theology, from the sending of Christ to an eschatological future in 1 Corinthians 15:24-28. Here Paul places even christological identity at the service of a *theocentric* vision.[7] When all things are indeed subjected to Christ, then "the Son himself will be subjected to him who put all things under him, *that God may be everything to everyone.*" Christ reorients us to God, to whom Christ himself, in typical kenotic fashion, continues to yield himself so that in the end God may be all in all.

This self-giving that stands at the center of God's revelation in Jesus Christ implies that our task as theologians and preachers is to find the words and images—already existing in our culture and language—that express the gospel so that it can be heard as good news spoken specifically to those who hear. To be sure, there are times when what we have available to us in language and culture seems to make the gospel harder to communicate, or even opposes it. Yet it is also true that the gospel, like Christ himself, keeps entering into human language and culture in a kind of self-effacing love. Like Christ, the gospel points in the end not to itself, but to the God who so loves the world in profligate self-giving.

Context in the Concrete

The question, then, for us is how to find the words and images that the Holy Spirit uses to make the gospel heard in our time and place. Clearly we need to understand more about context in order to bring it into such difficult conversation with the gospel. One well-known tool in the Canadian context is a book called *Getting Started on Social Analysis in Canada.*[8] At the beginning of the book the authors invite the readers to interpret their context from something as simple as a cup of coffee. How are matters of context revealed through a shared cup of coffee? The authors point to the many relationships that impinge on such a coffee-shop moment. Start with the coffee beans and start to ask questions: Who grew them? Under what conditions were they produced? How well were the producers paid for the labor? Who made it possible for someone to bring this product to North America? Once here, who packaged and distributed the product that found its way into your cup? Did the coffee product arrive by truck? How did the local vendor obtain the product they sold to you? Are you sitting in a Starbucks or in a mom-and-pop coffee shop hanging on for dear life on a street corner in some forgotten town? How was your coffee brewed—with a filter bleached by the addition of whitening chemicals? Who brought you your coffee—a person working for minimum wage or perhaps a small-businessperson? What was your coffee brought in—a porcelain cup made in the developing world or a Styrofoam cup whose production has an impact on the very environment in which we live? Did you add cream or creamer? If it's the former, what kind of subsidies or marketingboard policies brought it to you in that little thimble-sized plastic cup; if it's the latter, just what kind of oils and emulsifiers in it make it dissipate and smooth out your coffee? There is, when you think about it, as the book *Getting Started* points out, a whole contextual world in something as simple and everyday as a cup of coffee.

To pay attention to context, therefore, is to consider several different aspects of our life together. The aspects are neither discrete nor easily separable. In fact, these different contextual features are more likely to interact. So when we think about context, we will be talking about matters like economic arrangements, culture, social relationships, the media and technology, the world of politics, and even ideology (in fact, matters of media and ideology, because of their cross-situational importance, will show up in more than one of the subsequent situational chapters). The goal here is not to give *the* definitive, exhaustive list. Rather, it is to help bring gospel and context into a more self-conscious relationship. Chances are, preachers do this all the time. Because of CPE, most pastors know that psychological matters of context need to be brought into conversation with the gospel in situations like visiting the sick, comforting the grieving, or even preparing a couple for marriage. Imagine, though, what the gospel looks like when we think about "visiting the sick" within the horizon of the economics of the health-care system, the political realities of public versus private health insurance (and who's actually covered or treated), or the problems of the health-care system with "disabling" professions[9] that treat patients as diseases rather than fully responsible persons. The point of contextual reflection with the gospel is to articulate the gospel more clearly for the particular elements of this time and place, for these particular persons.

Context is in actuality what you see, perceive, and interpret—and then some. Because we are creatures shaped by our time and place, by the "isms" and "ologies" that dominate our lives, we are frequently unaware of context. Like the fish swimming in clear water in a fishbowl and breathing in oxygen through the gills as it swims through the transparent liquid, we may not see the way in which our context orients and grounds our lives. We "live from" these attitudes, perspectives, and unspoken realities but rarely stop to think about their impact on us. At the risk of mixing metaphors, consider how a context may be a bit like a tree. Above ground are leaves, branches, and a trunk—all of which we can observe when we really stop to look instead of speeding by a landscape in our cars. Yet there is much beneath the ground that we don't see: the ground and the roots that give the tree stability and life.[10] Doing situational preaching that accounts for relating gospel to context requires a view that sometimes considers the otherwise invisible "air we breathe" or, conversely, looks not just at the visible tree, but considers the roots and ground underneath. Contexts are complex and changing. However, situational preaching does itself no favor unless it understands more deeply and more complexly the elements of context and how they shape any moment of gospel proclamation.

Because of this complexity, both of us like aspects of a praxis model of theological reflection that Bob calls "the theological spiral." Like the praxis model described above, it views theological reflection as a process of movement. While it starts with the gospel, it moves more deeply toward the world *and* the theological tradition. Because it is a process of change, there is no mere circling back, let alone changeless identities. In fact, the process drives us back to hear the gospel and frees us in ever-spiraling ways to live it out more fully. The diagram we use in our class looks like this:

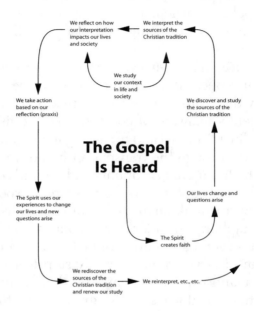

We reflect on how our interpretation impacts our lives and society

We interpret the sources of the Christian tradition

We study our context in life and society

We take action based on our reflection (praxis)

We discover and study the sources of the Christian tradition

The Gospel Is Heard

The Spirit uses our experiences to change our lives and new questions arise

Our lives change and questions arise

The Spirit creates faith

We rediscover the sources of the Christian tradition and renew our study

We reinterpret, etc., etc.

Here, clearly, gospel and context interrelate, spiraling onward as new situations present themselves for theologically informed action.

Gospel and Situation

In moving from context to situation, we are in one sense moving from the general to the specific. The context is that within which things happen and are interpreted. A situation is that which happens and is interpreted. The context is the framework of ideas, beliefs, and attitudes that we inhabit; a situation is an event to which we bring that framework. The context is the atmosphere; a situation happens within the atmosphere.

We have already described briefly that the kinds of situations the gospel addresses in preaching are likely of at least two specific types: limit moments and decision moments. David Buttrick has argued that such situations are important for gospel address because they either provoke questions of transcendence (limit) or lead to questions of divine purpose such that we question who we are and what we are to do (decision). Beyond that, he argues that those situations that "connect with profound onto-logical or historical questions" concern themselves with "crucial questions of meaning and morality" and "fit into the structures of Christian consciousness," which means that they allow for a distinction between our twofold reality of a "being-saved" community, which at the same time has a sense of "being-in-the world."[11] These understandings of situation help us discern whether a situation of limit or decision is of sufficient weight for pulpit address.

We tend to think that such moments also call into ques-tion two other important realities that Buttrick himself does not explicitly name. On the one hand, it could be argued that such moments call the gospel itself into question. In the face of death, tragedy, or crisis, for example, we bump not only into the limits of our finitude and grope toward God, but we also call the gospel into question. How can we make sense of the gospel that grounds our life together in the face of such limit moments? Similarly, such moments also call into question our own self-understanding in Lutheran theology as *simul justus et peccator,* simultaneously justified and yet sinners. There is in such moments a temptation to view ourselves as either more or less than we actually are. In limit and decision moments, it may just be that something central to the gospel message and our paradoxical self-understanding of ourselves as justified and yet sinners is at stake.

Naturally, our personal involvement makes determination difficult. As a practical matter of congregational leadership, we preachers will not always know for sure what to do: speak of a situation privately with those affected, mention the situation in the prayers to bring it before the congregation and God, or in some cases decide to preach a situational sermon. We pastors are still human beings and subject to the same vicissitudes as every-one else on this whirling earth. We also find ourselves numbed and silenced in the face of public crises and at times reduced to tears at a shared tragic loss. Yet our pain can also help us see where and why the gospel word needs to be spoken in a given situation. David's wife is a pastoral psychotherapist. When she works through something difficult with a client, she has been taught to "move toward the resistance." Maybe that is what we are charged to do—to speak with our all-too-human lips a word of gospel even when situations open up into the yawning chasm of the abyss.

In the face of such difficulties, theologians can give us more than a little guidance. Edward Farley speaks of our very problem in his groundbreaking article on "Interpreting Situations."[12] Farley acknowledges the complexity of situations and helps describe interpreting situations as a "theological hermeneutic."[13] First, we are to identify a situation and describe its "distinctive and constituent features." This is no small task, as Farley notes, as situations are more than objects, but multidimensional realities in which we live. Second, we need to understand that every situation has a past. Situations can be the result of past events, many aspects of which we are not even aware, let alone have dealt with. Situations do not just emerge *ex nihilo*; they have a history. Third, situations happen within other situations. To speak of a reality close to home as if it had no connection to greater worldwide realities would be to live in a contrived local fiction. Fourth, theological discernment must not only be present throughout the first three steps, but *central* at the end. Why? For Farley the nature of a situation is that it places us in a moment of demand and response. It is no neutral series of objects to be described and merely noted. Because of this, Farley describes the theological task of reflecting on situations this way:

> A theological version of this task cannot avoid the insights of its own mythos into the corruption and redemption of human beings. Because of that corruption, human beings shape the demand of the situation according to their idolatries, their absolutized self-interests, their ethnocentrisms, their participations in structures of power. Faith, then

interprets situations and their demands as always contain-
ing this element of corruption and redemption. Situations
pose to human beings occasions for idolatry and redemption. The discernment of the demand-response is at the
very heart of a theological hermeneutic of situations.[14]

With situations, something is at stake. At such points we
need much more than a hermeneutic of texts. We need a theological hermeneutic of situations. We need a gospel word born
of theological insight.

CHAPTER 3

PREACHING GOSPEL AT FUNERALS

M ost pastors remember their first funeral. Bob's first was the funeral of a stillborn baby. What he remembers most clearly is following the funeral director from the chapel to the grave with the director carrying a small white coffin and having no idea what to say to parents who had just seen their hopes and dreams for this child dashed in a horrifying and unexpected end to nine months of anticipation. He also remembers a desire not to say something dishonest or trite—there is just something not right, and something that cannot be put right, about a much-wanted and much-anticipated child not being given a chance at life.

In situations like these, every pastor and every congregation knows that funeral sermons are important. People come to funerals expecting to hear something that helps them make sense of the fact that every life ends in death, that helps them to make sense of the particular life and death of the person being buried, and that helps them make sense of their own life and eventual death. People may be more open and more vulnerable at funerals than at any other time. They may also be more closed and defensive, so the preacher needs to be able to read the situation and speak the gospel as clearly and explicitly as possible. In particular, the preacher dare not offer syrup when spinach is needed, dare not give in to the temptation to substitute culturally approved sentimentality or moralism for a clear word of God's unconditional promise.

Discerning the Context

Bob had the privilege of growing up in Southern California, where the modern funeral industry took shape. He remembers a day late in the summer of 1964, just before reading Evelyn Waugh's *The Loved One* in his senior high school English class, when he and a friend had been taken to Forest Lawn, Southern California's most famous mega-cemetery, to see the huge window and painting that attracted tourists from around the world. The friend had only recently arrived from Brazil to spend the year and was very homesick, so the two teenagers were looking a bit down in the mouth as they walked through the mausoleum. A security guard noticed them and said, "Smile, boys. This is a happy place!" Even then this comment struck Bob as odd. Neither of us is quite sure how a large space in which one is surrounded by decomposing corpses stacked eight or ten high could be "happy," but that is the mind-set of the modern funeral industry. Death is the one thing that is never mentioned.

And make no mistake, the modern American and Canadian funeral happens in the midst of a major industry that dominates contemporary funeral customs. Like almost everything else in a consumer society like ours, funerals, cremations, and burials are commodities that are marketed to consumers using sophisticated techniques, often by large corporations.[1] Pastors are very much a part of this economic machinery. Clergy are what is known in the funeral industry as "cash advance items," that is, third-party service providers. The funeral home collects a fee from the family of the dead person and passes a portion of that along to the service provider. In addition, clergy are one of the prime targets of funeral industry marketers, even as leaders of the funeral industry see clergy as potential spoilers of profit for their possibly recommending lower-cost funeral options. That means that it is incumbent on the contemporary North American pastor to be as aware as possible of the marketing techniques of the average funeral director and the practices of the funeral industry in general.

A good place to start is with Jessica Mitford's *The American Way of Death Revisited*, the 1998 revision of her 1963 classic.[2] In the early 1960s Mitford set out to explore how the act of burying the dead had become a major industry. What she found confirmed the suspicions of many, sent a tremor of fear through the industry, and lead to a variety of regulations on the state and federal level in the United States. It also gave impetus to the growth of "memorial societies" in the United States and Canada. In the mid-1990s Mitford decided once again to survey the industry to see what had changed in the previous thirty years. The product of her research was every bit as damning as it had been in the '60s, with the added abuses that flow from concentration in the industry. This time there was no response of further regulation. Government was in the hands of people hell-bent to deregulate, and many states had even disbanded the agencies responsible for regulating and inspecting funeral homes and cemeteries. As a result there was also not much fear on the part of the industry—the funeral directors and cemetery owners had learned how to market their way around the public's desire for cheaper, simpler funeral customs.

What we think of as the typical modern North American funeral and cemetery are not old and honored traditions. Prior to the nineteenth century, graveyards or burial grounds were rather unkempt and dismal places. In some growing cities the burying ground was simply a vacant lot at the edge of town that later got covered over by buildings of whatever sort were needed to accommodate business or population. The first modern cemetery—a word coined for the occasion—was Mount Auburn in Boston, which opened in 1831 and soon became a tourist attraction and destination for middle- and upper-class Bostonians. While The New Burying Ground in New Haven, Connecticut, is a generation older, it is Mount Auburn, the first graveyard designed to look like a park, which is really the distant ancestor of Forest Lawn.[3] Mount Auburn set the standard that a modern, parklike cemetery ought not just be a burying ground for the dead, but also a source of moral uplift for the living. From suburban Boston such "rural cemeteries" spread throughout North America, eventually reaching their zenith at Forest Lawn in Glendale, California. More recently a new twist on the park cemetery has emerged, derived from Forest Lawn's practice of drawing curious visitors to see its wonders: the cemetery as tourist attraction.

Bob's wife Nancy grew up in Hollywood, California, where her parents and grandparents are buried. The cemetery there, which backs on to an old movie studio, has always been something of a draw for those who wanted to see—as a wandering tourist once put it to Bob's mother-in-law—"where the famous bodies are." Cult followers appear at certain gravesites every year on the long-dead star's birthday. The old Hollywood Memorial Park had fallen on hard times since it was in a changing, multi-ethnic neighborhood and not able to compete with the newer cemeteries in the suburbs. The strip of land along Santa Monica Boulevard had even been sold off for a strip mall. Then the cemetery was purchased by Brent and Tyler Cassity[4] and a newer, better, more tourist-friendly incarnation arose: "Hollywood Forever." Now there is a Web site (where you can view "eternal" online memorials, a Cassity innovation) and upbeat brochures featuring the Greek temple gravesite of one of the movies' early swashbucklers. Of course, the tourists don't pay the freight, so prices have to rise to accommodate all of the spiffy new facilities, and customers are encouraged to add on as many extra-price options as possible. Revenues have grown from a measly sixteen thousand dollars in 1997 (the last year of the old operation) to over nine million in 2005.[5] The Cassitys would agree with Stewart Enterprises chairman Frank B. Stewart Jr., who concluded that "so-called 'heritage' cemeteries—those steeped in tradition and consisting of crypts and plots owned by thousands of prominent families—represented an ideal base from which to market the complete range of options provided by death care facilities now known as combined operations."[6] Not every cemetery can be the burial place of old Hollywood's elite, but this same pattern is occurring in older commercial cemeteries across the continent.

Meanwhile, even municipal cemeteries do their best to look like the commercial leaders of the industry.

The modern version of the undertaker, the professional "funeral director," began to come into being at the beginning of the twentieth century. Among the ancients only the Egyptians were much given to preserving the dead chemically. The practice of embalming, while never completely disappearing, had been given up even in Egypt after the majority of the population had converted to Christianity in the late Greco-Roman period. Occasionally kings and emperors would be embalmed for various reasons of state. The most curious case of embalming was in 1775 when Martin Van Butchell had his wife embalmed and preserved in their drawing room so that he could continue to spend her money. The first widespread use of embalming in the United States was during the Civil War when entrepreneurs at the battlefront would embalm dead soldiers and ship them home to their families for $100. In 1900, around the time that undertakers were first called "funeral directors," embalming was still the exception and, when done, was done in the home. The use of coffins was not widespread until the nineteenth century, and even then the most common receptacle was the "plain pine box" with little or no ornamentation. While metal "caskets"—a word little used before the last several generations—were known in the first half of the nineteenth century, they were resisted and little used until the 1920s.[7]

These two practices, embalming and decorative coffins, are the bedrock of the funeral industry and, outside of the cemetery plot, make up the major part of funeral expenses. When, in reaction to the first edition of Mitford's *The American Way of Death,* people began to seek cremation in place of burial, the industry maintained its position by convincing people that, cremation or no, embalming and an expensive casket were still necessary. Today a funeral with cremation is just as expensive as a funeral with burial. The social and cultural context for any funeral sermon includes a particular culture's attitudes toward death and practices around death and funerals. The new "cemeterians" and funeral directors represent the direction in which our culture's beliefs about death are intersecting with consumer capitalism to change the nature of the modern funeral. For the foreseeable future, funerals will continue to be occasions when people show their social class through the expense of the coffin, flowers, and arrangements. Pastors are now and will continue to be under pressure to conform to the commodity form of funerals in a consumer society. It takes courage, pastoral skill, and an act of cultural resistance to preach a sermon and conduct a funeral that communicates an authentic word of gospel in such a context.

Discerning the Situation

Among the most painful funerals to witness are those where the one who is presiding minister and preacher either appears to know nothing at all about the deceased or obviously claims to know the dead person much better than he or she really did. Such practices rightly irritate gospel preachers *and* hearers! No doubt, within our cultural context each particular funeral has certain cultural commonalities. Yet each funeral is as unique as the particular person who has died. When preparing the funeral sermon we need to keep both the commonalities and uniquenesses in mind.

While each death and each funeral is unique, there are characteristics of certain deaths that mean that similar questions might be asked and certain issues be present. For example, in cases of death by suicide, many times the family will ask why they did not see it coming or what they should have done to prevent the death. Some of these "types" of funerals include: death of an aged saint, a child, or a young person; suicide; tragic or sudden death; deaths of an entire group (e.g., in an earthquake or flood); victim of violence; war casualties; lingering deaths, such as from cancer; death of someone estranged from family or community; and "media-event" deaths. Again, within each type there are commonalities even as each funeral is unique.

The demographics of the congregation one serves will influence which sorts of funerals one does more often. For example, Bob served two congregations, one of which was in a newer neighborhood with mostly younger members and the other of which was in an older neighborhood with mostly older members. The funerals in the former congregation were all for children, young people, people who had died in an accident, and people who had died in middle age of cancer or heart attacks. The funerals in the other congregation were all of people who died in old age. Bob's wife, Nancy, served as pastor to a refugee community where most of her "funerals" were memorial services for relatives who had been killed or died back home. Her parishioners, being political refugees, could not return home to attend the funeral.

Neither of us claims to be an expert in pastoral care, so this section will not be a mini-lecture on grief or bereavement counseling. There is a huge literature on the subject of grief with which every pastor should be familiar.[8] However, the pastor should not take on the sort of professional role that disables the natural response of the community. In a 1984 essay, "John Deere and the Bereavement Counselor," John McKnight compares the professionalization of people's grief to the action of the steel plow on the prairies of Sauk County, Wisconsin. McKnight notes that in the beginning, just after John Deere invented the tool in 1837, the steel plow helped European pioneers cut through the prairie sod that had stumped their older iron plows, and for a time the soil was rich and the harvests abundant. But each year the land became a little bit less able to support the kind of agriculture that the steel plow encouraged. After thirty years the land was exhausted and the farmers moved further west, seeking new lands to plow.[9] By the 1930s they had turned places like Oklahoma and Saskatchewan into dust bowls.

McKnight goes on to show how the introduction of professional technologies of care such as bereavement counseling can erode the traditional ways in which cultures have dealt with grief for millennia. What he calls "the community of mourners" can break down, sometimes quite quickly, under the onslaught of professionals.[10] So we give you this caution: professionals, such as pastors, can easily disempower people in the name of helping. This is not to say that pastors ought not care skillfully. It is to say that gospel ministry is not about creating a "culture of therapy"; nor is it about substituting a "therapeutic relationship" for a pastoral one. Tools are probably necessary, but some tools we use can become impediments to gospel community. This is just the opposite of the priesthood of all believers. Part of the task of the preacher of the gospel is to be a tool through which the good news of what God has done in Christ empowers people to live as a community of Jesus' disciples in the midst of the world community. The role of the church as the disciple community[11] in the world is to direct us all toward the reign of God where none will be professionals but all will be true amateurs, that is, people who do what they do out of love.

The task of the one who is called to preach the gospel at funerals is also, while being present with people in their grief, to listen carefully for the theology that they express. One might hear profound expressions of gospel faith, of complete trust in the grace of God. These can become part of what helps the preacher find an appropriate expression of the gospel in a specific funeral sermon. One might also hear some understandings of God and God's relationship with people that contradict any notion of a gracious and loving God. Sometimes people might even prefer an arbitrary, cruel god in the face of an inscrutable death ("I guess the Lord just called him home"), out of desire to make at least some sense, even if that god sounds little like the God revealed in Jesus Christ.

The midst of grief is not the best time to "correct" the grieving person's theological errors, but it is a good time to listen carefully and pastorally for the grieving person's "default" theology, the deep, perhaps unconscious beliefs that are shaped into us through hundreds of dimly remembered conversations or events from our past. These come out when our rational guard is down because of some trauma. They may appear as offhand remarks or as a searching response to events beyond explanation. Most of the time we would all prefer that things make sense, that there be some meaning, and often we are more willing to accept a "bad" meaning than no meaning. The absurdity of life is a bit much to accept. Discerning the situation means to be listening for these revelations from our subrational vault of beliefs. The gospel preacher can hear both what is said and hear the quest for meaning in the midst of seeming absurdity that undergirds what is said so as to craft a sermon that gently leads hearers to an appreciation for the meaning of grace.

How default theologies come out and which default theologies come out will depend on the circumstances of death and the relationship between the person who has died and those who mourn. In deaths "out of season," such as the death of a child or young person or an accidental death, we come face-to-face with the transitory nature of life in a much more profound way than we do at the death of an aged pillar of the church. We might well hear some say something like, "Well, I guess that God needed her more than we do," or "God must have a good reason for taking him." The theology of either of these statements is suspect, but both are also symptoms of the search for meaning in the face of an event that has threatened all of our usual assumptions and expectations for life. In such a case the funeral sermon should directly address the meaning questions that surround a death out of time—questions that also, we should remember, accompany any death, but in a less obvious way—while respecting the needs of the grieving person. We may also need to find some forceful way to deal with the "Job's friends" who are not themselves directly involved but who want to be helpful by making inane statements about the meaning of life and death.

Gospel Commonplaces for Funeral Sermons

Commonplace One:
The gospel claims that God is gracious even in the face of death.

The altarpiece of the City Church in Wittenberg by Lucas Cranach the Younger is a graphic depiction of Luther's theology of word and sacrament. The predella shows Luther preaching from the pulpit on the left with the congregation standing (as was the custom of the time) on the right. In between them is a crucifix—a fairly graphic representation of Jesus dying on the cross. The preacher is gesturing toward the crucifix, drawing the congregation's attention to the dying Christ. In Luther's view this is the function of the sermon, to make the cross of Christ present for the congregation, to be part of the Holy Spirit making Christ's cross our cross. That is what we mean when we say that the task of all preaching is to articulate the gospel. Every sermon should make what God has done in Christ real for the congregation.

When we find ourselves in a tight spot we tend to revert to *our* "default" theology. For most of us, this is the theology that we have unconsciously learned from the time of infancy. Since in English-speaking North American culture this default is shaped by the gospel of hard work and positive thinking, when we revert to our default theology, we are likely to say something that sounds more like Horatio Alger Jr. or Norman Vincent Peale than it sounds like the good news of what God has done in Christ. That is problematic anytime, but it is especially problematic at funerals.

Here we have a unique preaching opportunity. By focusing on the gospel, we are offering nothing less than grace in the shadow of death. Funeral sermons are never just about what the deceased did, or even how we the bereaved now feel. These realities of life and grief are, rather, necessarily related to the gospel good news of God in Christ. Here preachers would be well advised to reflect on what God has done and is doing. Even at funerals, it is our theological task to "name God into the world" *in light of* this person's death and our human grief.

Implication—Since a funeral sermon should articulate the gospel in the light of human lives, it should say much more than merely a personal eulogy.

The task of making what God has done in Christ present for the congregation includes funeral sermons. A funeral sermon is not a eulogy; that is, the point of the sermon is not to praise the dead person. This is not to say we must say nothing good about the deceased, but we need to be very, very careful that we do not imply by our words or manner that it was or is that person's character or actions that is the basis for one's relationship with the ultimate ground of being, which in many people's default theology is connected with the act of eulogizing. To preach in such a fashion is the grossest sort of confusion of law and gospel. The point of a funeral sermon is to remind us all that the meaning of who we are, the life we have lived, and what the destiny of our lives has been and will be is found in the death and resurrection of Jesus of Nazareth and has been given to us as unconditional promise. Since a funeral sermon arises out of the intersection of the gospel and the specific situation, gospel proclamation happens in light of the actual life that is being remembered without making that life the source of anyone's salvation.

The gospel to be spoken is not the false promise that everything will work out all right in the end. The gospel is the word of the cross. Think for a moment about the funeral of a young spouse and parent who has died of cancer. The role of pastor and preacher can be complicated by the desire of those left behind to see the one who has died as a heroic or saintly figure. In such a case articulating the gospel means that we do not fall into the trap of eulogizing someone who might well deserve a eulogy, but, rather, provide a space where anger at God or existential confusion in the face of an untimely death can be spoken as part of the gospel promise. Depending on the circumstances of the situation, the sermon at such a funeral might well include a gospel-centered "I don't know why this happened." This does not mean, of course, that there is no place for eulogy in the funeral service, but that it needs to be kept distinct from preaching the gospel. For instance, in our community, as in many others, the current custom is that members of the family or friends give a "remembrance" of the deceased.

Commonplace Two:
We humans are simul justus et peccator,[12] and the gospel of God's unconditional love for creation addresses us as we are.

This locus, or gospel commonplace, follows from the first. Precisely because the task of funeral preaching is speaking gospel in the light of real life and actual death, we are free and we are bound to tell the truth. Precisely because of the way Jesus lived and died, there is no need to sugarcoat any life or the sum of lives. God's grace is for sinners, not for the perfect. Christ's healing is for the sick, not the healthy. Precisely because the crucifixion of Jesus is at the center of Christian faith we can face deep confusion and even hopelessness with eyes wide open. Precisely because it is the story of what God has done in Christ that is central to gospel preaching, we can tell real stories and not Disneyfied versions of people's lives.

Not everyone will welcome the good news. Some us are so committed to the ideology of consumer capitalism that we insist on believing that we can lift ourselves up by our own bootstraps. Some of us have learned to cope with our lives by pretending that everything is really okay. Some of us have to wear rose-colored glasses in order to survive. In any of these cases and others, the gospel can be heard as threat. The focus of the funeral sermon always remains the gospel, but the pastoral preacher will want to discern how the gospel can be best heard in the particular situation. Just remember that the gospel plus a little bit of law equals soft law—which sounds gracious but is really just wishy-washy moralism. When we preach soft law, we are often popular, but we are never truthful.

David remembers the layout of his last church in New Johnsonville, Tennessee. The A-frame church featured a large glass wall at the back of the chancel. While people worshiped, heard God's living word, and received the means of grace at the table, they could look out the clear-glass portion of the wall. Interestingly, the transparent portion you could actually see through was cruciform. Why? Perhaps it is because only *through* the cross we Christians see clearly the world, life and death, as it really is.

Implication—We will not preach people into heaven or hell.

When we eulogize someone as a saint, we run the risk of trying to justify those whom God has already accepted in love. Sermons should deal with people as they really are and ultimately point to God's love for us in Christ—speak the truth in love.

You may have already had the experience of conducting the funeral for someone whose life was less than exemplary and/or whose way of being inflicted considerable pain on family members. Some members of the family may want to sugarcoat the truth; others may be completely alienated and avoid the funeral altogether. Some will want to forgive and forget (perhaps for good or not-so-good reasons), while others are still far too hurt to even consider forgiving.

In such a case pastoral discretion is essential, but what family members need most to hear is the gospel, not false optimism or harsh condemnation. Preaching the gospel does not mean using the funeral as an opportunity for an old-fashioned, "hellfire and brimstone" blast against evil and call to "repentance." Such a sermon is not heard as gospel—in large part because it is heavy on law and very, very short on good news—and may very well be abusive. At the same time, such a funeral sermon is not the time for cheap universalism either. To say to someone who has, for example, been abused by an alcoholic father that such a person has "gone to heaven" is not good news for the living any more than hellfire and brimstone. Such a funeral should remain the existential struggle that it really is for the people who are experiencing the death of someone whose meaning for them is deeply problematic.

> ### Commonplace Three:
> *The focus of God's address to us in word and sacrament is on God's acts for us, not our acts for God.*

Sometimes it is hard to remember in the moment, but a funeral is a worship service, a liturgical act in which God's people hear God's word, pray, praise, and give thanks. The funeral liturgy is a unique and "occasional" service, but it is a liturgy. One implication of this affirmation is that funeral liturgies and funeral sermons should do what every liturgy and every sermon should do: focus on what God has done in the life, death, resurrection, and ascension of Jesus. The word of God and the sacraments are about God, not about us. The gospel is the plumb line for all liturgies and all sermons, as it is for funerals. Worship is always about the gospel in dialogue with broken-yet-redeemed creation, as are funerals. The unique characteristic of funerals is that they occur in the context of remembering and mourning a specific broken-yet-redeemed human.

One way in which this liturgical reality immediately becomes clear is in the relationship of the funeral to baptism. In baptism we die to ourselves and begin living into the promise of resurrection (Romans 6). The use of a funeral pall on a casket is designed to be reminiscent of this reality. This death needs to be seen in light of the death already begun at baptism, yet the white pall also points to a divine promise: that the good news here in the face of death is what God promises to do. From the day we wear a white garment at our baptism to the day a white pall covers our body, our hope is not in ourselves, but in the promise of God. It is this hope that has been animating us—who have died already in baptism—toward the "not-yet" promise of resurrection life. Ever since we died in baptism, we've been living only on God's promise. In the shadow of our final death, we are covered by that promise alone. Even in death we are "with God" because of what God has done in the death and resurrection of Christ.

> **Implication**—A funeral sermon should focus on God's action for us, rather than our action for God. The latter runs the risk of works righteousness and fails to announce the gospel.

The gospel is about what God has done for us, not about what we do for God. Funeral sermons can inadvertently communicate that the focus is reversed by laying claim to the deceased person's good works and/or by implying that the deceased is surely with God because the deceased was such a good person. We might even subtly claim that the deceased is surely with God because the deceased was so hard to get along with, creating sort of a "salvation by bad works" model! Most of us will avoid the more obvious temptations here, but we will probably still speak about the witness of certain people we bury. Here we need to be especially careful. Even when the deceased actually was a powerful witness to the unconditional grace of God in Christ, because of the beliefs of our society, it is incredibly easy for people to hear that the deceased is with God *because* the deceased was such a good witness. What we want people to hear is that we are all with God because of *God's* witness and actions.

One way to check our sermons is through a simple grammatical test: Who or what is the subject of the majority of the sentences? If "I" or the deceased is the subject most of the time, then there is trouble for sure. If God is the subject most of the time, then we are starting down the right path.

> ## Commonplace Four:
> *God's revelation in Christ limits what we can claim to know about God and the future.*

We must be modest about what we claim. Any attributions of divine wrath and judgment in death will always be limited because of God's revelation of self-giving love in Jesus Christ. The funeral sermon must not presume to know more than any of us can of a soul's eternal destiny apart from God's continuing unconditional love for us made known through Christ. This is the "eschatological reservation."

Granting that Christian theologians for many centuries believed that the idea of the immortality of the soul was an orthodox doctrine and that people who hold this doctrine believe that certain passages in the New Testament support their views, most exegetes and theologians are now more convinced by the text of Scripture and the bare words of the Apostles' Creed: we believe in the resurrection of the body. As a result, we do not preach the immortality of the human soul, but the eternality and unrelenting nature of God's love for us in life, death, and beyond death—prototypically related to us in the life, death, and resurrection of Jesus Christ, who is the firstfruits of God's new creation. Christian eschatology is about what God is doing to make creation right; it is not about the eternal cycles of the ages. Funeral sermons should point the hearers forward to the coming reign of God in which we shall all together stand before the face of a gracious and loving God.

Implication—We should not attribute someone's death to God's will or act.

Here our intent is not to argue with classic Reformed theologies of the sovereignty of God's grace, but precisely to affirm grace over against law-based understandings of God. To say that God is directly responsible for a specific death is presumptuous. It also assumes God is just an arbitrary sovereign, rather than the God revealed to us in Jesus Christ. Here is where listening for the default theology of the mourners is important. What kind of comments do people make about the person's death? Often the preacher can hear people's default theology more clearly in offhand comments than in direct counseling or other more formal settings. In an attempt to find some meaning in the face of death, especially an unexpected or tragic death, people might well prefer an arbitrary or vengeful God to the possibility that life is just absurd. It may seem counterintuitive, but sometimes the gospel preacher's task is to affirm the absurdity of it all. Our hope for our hearers is that they be given the gift of faith in God's grace even when all of the evidence is to the contrary. Part of living that hope is the preacher being honest about the evidence in a way that helps hearers embrace both reality and trust in God.

Perhaps helpful here is the distinction Luther makes between the hidden God and the revealed God when he talks about pre-destination. There are things that God has revealed to us in the gospel in Scripture. God has promised to be gracious. God wills the salvation of all. We are given the promise of salvation in Christ's death and resurrection. God's power and wisdom are expressed as weakness and foolishness. This is the basis of our hope in Christ. At the same time, there are things that God has not revealed, things that God has graciously kept hidden from our understanding. These are best left alone. Speculation about the hidden God in the end only leads people into despair. Talk of God's will or act in a specific death is rank speculation about the workings of the hidden God. It is not a word of grace in the face of a tragic death.

Implication—We should not presume to say "someone is in heaven."

Though it may not seem so, to say that someone is in heaven is as presumptuous as saying that a person is in hell. We cannot know any specific person's eternal destiny; we can only hope and trust that God is gracious. We know that the gospel reveals God's love for us and God's commitment to relationship with us. We cling to the hope that God's grace will, in the end, win out over sin, death, and evil, but we always need remember that this is hope in a promise, not resting on a guarantee. As Paul says, now we see through a glass darkly, but then we shall see face-to-face.

There will be cases where mourners are quite agitated by this question. This will depend on the values of the community and the individual. In some cases the preacher may need to confront legalistic attitudes, though this should always be done gently, though without compromise, in a funeral sermon. In such cases one might remind the hearers of God's gracious will for the salvation of all and remind people that, as Paul says in 1 Corinthians 1 and 2, God's powerful will to save is sometimes expressed as weakness or foolishness. The question for a preacher is always, "How can I be an instrument through which people might hear the gospel?" In a case where people are agitated about the deceased's eternal destiny, the gospel will always be a word of hope, but it can never be a blanket assurance.

Implication—Preachers should find pastorally sensitive ways of articulating theology consistent with the gospel.

The point is not to be theologically correct for the sake of mere correctness. Make no mistake, we want to encourage well-thought-out, gospel-centered orthodoxy. In fact, we are convinced that good theology, a theology that takes death and resurrection seriously, is more likely to be pastorally helpful. At the same time, we all know about pastors—ourselves included, of course!—who get far too hung up on "true doctrine." And we have seen how people shut down their ears when they hear us being nitpickers. We always need to remember that the gospel intends to be pastorally helpful to people. So don't use grief counseling as a time to correct people's false doctrine about heaven, hell, the end-times, or the immortality of the soul.

At the same time, don't make any statements yourself that would lead people toward theologies that are less than healthy, less than gospel centered, and less than orthodox. Remember, too, what "orthodox" really means. Truly orthodox theology has always evolved and been revised so that the gospel can be heard as good news in the present cultural and linguistic context. The goal is theology that communicates the gospel to people here and now. Avoid theology that is legalistic, trendy, or unintelligible. The point of good theology is that people, through hope in the truth of the gospel, can live truthful lives. False theologies lead to false hopes and false lives—and no one is ever helped by false hopes. Preachers are to be heralds of the truth of God's unconditional promise in the death and resurrection of Jesus Christ. That truth is most assuredly helpful and pastoral indeed.

> ## Commonplace Five:
> *We take death seriously because of the centrality of Christ's cross in revealing God to us.*

One of us once had a colleague who seemed to have a never-ending supply of euphemisms for death. No one in the congregation ever died. They "passed over," they "ended their temporal journey," they were "now in the eternal presence," but none of them ever died. There is really no need for Christian preachers to try to cover up the truth that we all die and that we have gathered at this particular moment in this particular place because one of us has died. Because Jesus has died, we can face reality. Because God in Christ has experienced death on the cross, we recognize how serious and yet how hopeful death is.

In this recognition we are flying in the face of many cultural attitudes and practices in North America. As a society we have more and more isolated death into an institutional setting in hospitals and nursing homes. People are beginning to resist by insisting on dying at home or in a hospice, but even hospice is an institutional response. Under the guidance of the funeral industry, funeral customs often try to disguise the fact that the "loved one" is actually dead. In this atmosphere preachers can bring a note of gospel honesty and hope by facing death seriously for what it really is.

One source of possibilities for facing death honestly is shown by Martin Luther's 1534 lectures on Psalm 90.[13] In this commentary Luther points out that death presents two faces to us, depending on the perspective we take. From the perspective of law, of conditional promises, death is terrifying and is the ultimate sign of our estrangement from God, the rest of creation, and ourselves. Death writes the final verdict on our attempts to perform and achieve our way into God's favor, and that verdict shows how wasted everything we have attempted really is. Thus, for each of us, no matter how pious, death is a revelation of the futility and hopelessness of life. From the perspective of the gospel, of God's unconditional promise in Christ, death is the beginning of eternal life. It is the point where we finally leave sin and futility behind. In death under the gospel God accepts us into our true home. What we have hoped for has come to pass in Christ. Thus, for each of us, death is the most beautiful revelation of God's grace and mercy and the true meaning and hope of life.

Anything we might say about death is always said in the midst of the existential tension that we live in light of both the law view and the gospel view of death at one and the same time. This existential dynamic cannot be resolved for any of us still living. The preacher cannot wish away either part of the tension. At the same time, it is our hope and trust that death under the law is penultimate and that the gospel perspective is ultimate. If it were not for the gospel, for Jesus' crucifixion we would have to find some way to hide the reality of death as law. Because of the gospel we can look at death with eyes wide open and thereby be better pastors for the dying and grieving.

> **Implication**—Funeral sermons should face death squarely in ways consistent with the pastoral relationship to the mourners and the grieving community.

The basic rule for preachers is: don't go beyond what you really know about people. If you don't know how people will take what you say, be cautious. In funeral preaching we should always err on the side of caution so that we do not hurt people any more than they are already hurt by the reality of death. This is not to say that we should get scared and fall back into the practice of using flowery euphemisms. It is to say that we are called to preach the gospel in ways that people can hear it as good news *for them*. What we try to avoid is people hearing what we say as bad news or failing to hear at all.

We should also say that, while preaching a gospel funeral sermon might have to be an act of cultural resistance, it must still be heard as good news in the context of the community that is mourning the particular death at hand. We dare not confuse unintelligibility with cultural resistance. People need to hear the good news in their own language. This becomes especially important when the community the preacher is serving is multicultural. The funeral sermon may have to become a translation for that portion of the congregation that is not familiar with the funeral practices of the family of the deceased so that all can see God's Spirit at work in their midst.

Conclusion

Because the medium of preaching is the oral word and our call is to preach, we use our language and the resources of story, image, and symbol in sermons for the sake of our hearers, that is, as a shared act of neighbor love in the very shadow of death. The funeral sermon is a sermon. This seeming tautology has at its core several affirmations. First, we want to affirm that the preacher should not think of what she or he does at funerals as a subgenre of the remembrances by family members. At the same time the preacher does not need to consider a funeral sermon as an afterthought or an annoyance to the mourners. This is a real sermon and should/can be considered as such. Second, and to repeat this point yet again, the funeral sermon is first of all about the gospel. The preacher will need to respect the customs of the community around funerals, but the preacher need not see those customs as a straitjacket but as a channel for gospel communication.

As a result, gospel preachers should allow their theology to come through as in their other preaching. They will attend to images that evoke loss and grief, as necessary. They will also attend to stories, metaphors, and images that begin to point to the shape of gospel promise: sometimes from a text, sometimes from a life as lived, sometimes from the shared promises that give us life in community (baptism, eucharist, etc.). Funeral preaching should be good gospel theology, but it ought not sound like a theological textbook. By using our words as an act of neighbor love, we also provide our hearers with something valuable. It is said that in some Orthodox churches a priest will stand at the entrance at the end of the service. As people leave, he hands out to each a piece of eucharistic bread. Some call it bread for the journey. By taking care with our language and being theologically evocative with it, perhaps we can offer mourners something similar in the very face of death.

Our task is to proclaim the gospel, and our tools are speech and language and all of the possibilities that spoken language opens up to us. We are free to make use of stories, images, symbols, analogies, and metaphors in any way that communicates the point. There is no need to be embarrassed to think about rhetorical tools and strategies in funeral sermons, for these tools and strategies are the means we use to preach the gospel. In fact, the funeral oration is one of the oldest forms of formal speech. We may not have the same goals as the orators at the funeral of some Greek general, but we do still stand in their shadow. Those orators understood that their words had power, and so should we.

Our task is neither to praise Caesar nor to bury him; our task is to hold up Christ as the hope of the living and the dead. In this task we can use stories from the deceased's life and people's memories of that life. We can use images suggested to us by conversations with the deceased before death or with mourners after death. We can draw on the store of cultural images and symbols as these support the fundamental task of gospel proclamation. The beauty of language can be put to good use in service of the central task.

We do not need to be embarrassed that words, speech, and language are the tools we have at our disposal. The funeral liturgy should leave times for silent prayer and thought, but the funeral sermon is not a time for trendy mysticism or wordless emoting from the preacher. Christians do not hold funerals in the dark, but in the light of the hope we have in Christ. That hope is expressed in the word—the WORD—of God. That word comes as *logos*, as speech that makes sense of the meaning of life in the face of death. The preacher is called to offer the gift of the gospel, incarnate in human language, to people who need something in which to hope. Preaching is always an act of neighbor love.

Use pastoral authority in this situation with great care. Temper the power given to you first and foremost with mercy and pastoral empathy. Again, the goal is not to be theologically "correct" but pastorally empathetic. Funerals are not a time for "Here I stand" moments. Funerals are a time for clear proclamation of the gospel in the midst of and for the sake of a grieving community.

CHAPTER 4

PREACHING GOSPEL AT WEDDINGS

Like so many church denominations these days, the denomination that we serve through our seminary (the Evangelical Lutheran Church in Canada) has spent a lot of time discussing marriage in relation to homosexuality. In Canada these issues are discussed a bit differently than they are in most of the United States, since same-sex marriage is legal in all of Canada. It is also the case in Canada generally and in the province where we live specifically that ordained clergy must hold a license issued by the provincial government in order to preside at marriages. Part of the process for receiving the license involves signing a statement that one will abide by all provincial laws regarding marriage. After years of our denomination saying that we could not consider pastors presiding at same-sex marriages, because this would violate the terms under which provincial licenses are issued, we now have to face the issue more directly. The debate has centered around the question of whether local congregations can make the decision for themselves whether their pastors may preside at marriage ceremonies for same-sex couples. In this debate members of the seminary faculties were asked to prepare a series of short essays on assigned topics for study by convention delegates. We were each assigned a topic and wrote an essay.[1]

In the course of researching and writing these essays, it became clear to us that what we had always just sort of assumed about weddings might not be quite right. We both received our theological education and served as parish pastors in the United States—Bob in California and David in South Dakota and Tennessee. In those states once you were ordained you just started doing weddings and signed your name on marriage licenses. In Ontario it has become much clearer to us that one really is acting as an officer of the province under the authority of a provincial license governed by acts of the provincial parliament and regulations of the provincial ministry. Pastors legalizing marriages—regardless of the gender mix of the couple—operate in an ambiguous, mixed role. The Canadian vocabulary makes this mixed role more obvious: Which ministry do we represent, the ministry of the gospel or the Ministry of Government Services and Consumer Affairs? For whom do we speak, God or the government?

Discerning the Context

Interestingly, Martin Luther favored making marriage matters strictly a concern of the secular authorities.[2] This is the result of the same theological move that removed marriage from the list of sacraments. It is not that marriage is not important, but that it is part of God's created order, not a part of the gospel that speaks the word of redemption in Christ to a fallen created order. An important corollary of Luther's doctrine of justification is what Charles Taylor calls "the affirmation of the ordinary."[3] According to Taylor, distinguishing between "ordinary life," the life of "production and reproduction, that is labour, the making of things needed for life, and our life as sexual beings, including marriage and the family,"[4] and the heroic life or the "good life" is deeply embedded in Greek thought. For Homer there are normal people and there are the heroes of *The Iliad and The Odyssey,* two quite different sorts of people. For Aristotle there is life—family, commerce, and labor—and there is the good life of deliberation about moral excellence and the order of things and the shaping and application of the laws of the polis. Aristotle sees everyday life as the infrastructure for the good life, but everyday life can never itself be the good life. The good life is for philosophers and rulers. Plato questioned whether the participation of leaders in government could be part of the good life. The Stoics went even further. They believed that the philosopher should be completely detached from labor, sexuality, and politics, which are adiaphora, indifferent things.

This distinction was picked up by Christianity at least as early as Clement of Alexandria and Origen, who distinguish everyday or "carnal" Christians who are content with the surface meaning of Scriptures and sacraments from contemplative or "spiritual" Christians who search for and understand the deeper meanings. Ideas of ascetic perfection and Greek views about the philosophic life became the breeding ground of the monastic sense of vocation, which supported a way of Christian life dependent on distinguishing perfect holiness from everyday holiness. The theological and spiritual writings of Christianity from 300 to 1500 are clearly based on the distinction of ordinary life from the good life. Even though in the Middle Ages marriage becomes a sacrament, it is still the second-best vocation, the vocation for those who cannot attain celibacy. Even among celibates, those who remain "in the world," that is, in parish churches, are second best to those who take up the vocation par excellence, monasticism. In fact, words such as *vocation, conversion,* and *religious* apply only to monastics.

> According to Taylor, the Reformation upsets these hierarchies, which displaces the locus of the good life from some special range of higher activities and places it within "life" itself. The full human life is now defined in terms of labour and production, on one hand, and marriage and family life on the other. At the same time the previous "higher" activities come under vigorous criticism.[5]

On the basis of the doctrine of justification, Luther seeks to abolish the boundary between the everyday life of production and reproduction and the good life of contemplation and holiness.

The Christian, justified by grace through faith, is called to be holy in the midst of everyday life, not apart from everyday life. For Luther, there is no distinction between the "secular" and the "religious," the monk and the shoemaker, the baptized and the ordained, the carnal and the Spirit-filled, the celibate and the married. For the justified sinner, all vocations are Christian vocations. There is no distinction between sacred and secular. Marriage, which had been a "second-best" vocation, now becomes a "second-to-none" vocation.

Specifically, this "affirmation that the fullness of Christian existence was to be found within the activities of this life, in one's calling and in marriage and the family"[6] results in several implications for our understanding of marriage. First, the importance of marriage is magnified, and magnified as something more than a release for sexual tensions. Marriage is a positive good, a vocation through which married people please God and do good works. Second, even though the importance and divine significance of marriage is enhanced, marriage is no longer considered a sacrament. Marriage is a gift of God the Creator as a secular vocation under the law for all humans, whether Christian or not. Luther understood sacraments as gifts of God the Redeemer in Christ as a means for communicating the grace of the gospel. Marriage is part of God's left-handed work; sacraments are part of God's right-handed work. Both are important, but they cannot be confused with one another. In fact, Luther saw the church's domination of marriage ceremonies and regulations as part of the medieval "Babylonian captivity," which required an act of liberation. In Luther's view, marriage could only be liberated from its medieval servitude if it became the responsibility of the state, God's chosen institution for the secular order, rather than the church, God's chosen institution for the spiritual order. Luther went so far as to say that pastors ought to have nothing to do with performing marriages or deciding who can or cannot get married.[7]

At the core of the ambiguity surrounding wedding sermons is the reality that there simply is no "biblical" theology of marriage. Of course, we know that many people believe that the

Scriptures have a theology of marriage, but when one actually looks at the text, one is hard pressed to identify just what that might be. The Bible spans cultural views of marriage from Solomon's thousand wives to the Pastoral Epistles' injunction that the congregational leader must be husband of only one wife to Paul's seeming preference that Christians not marry in light of the imminent parousia. Even the command in Exodus not to commit adultery must be read in light of the story of Judah and Tamar in Genesis. Stanley Hauerwas is quite right when he says, "The first enemy of the family is the church."[8] Throughout its history, from Jesus' saying, "Whoever comes to me and does not hate father and mother, wife and children, brothers and sisters, yes, and even life itself cannot be my disciple" (Luke 14:26), Christianity has been ambiguous at best about marriage and family. We simply cannot make credible claims to represent some sort of "biblical" or "traditional" form of marriage and family.

Many of us respond to this ambiguity by becoming breezy chaplains of the status quo who wallow in the romanticism of the consumer-capitalist wedding (an idea of marriage based on nineteenth-century ideals) or by becoming crotchety liturgical purists who insist that only "sacred" music can be used and every aspect of the wedding must be "Christian." The latter approach is reminiscent of a neighborhood scold who complains about boys walking by on the sidewalk whistling dirty tunes—when you stop to think about it, it doesn't make much sense. Because of our own ambiguous role in weddings as officers of the state as well as ministers of the gospel, we really have no standing from which to throw stones at the "secularity" of anyone else.

This is not to say that the church has not, over the centuries, done some reflection on the meaning of marriage. In many cases such reflection has mirrored the morals and values of whatever the society of the time and place thought, but in significant cases the reflection of the church ran quite counter to the attitudes, common assumptions, and mores of the surrounding society.[9] As Hauerwas points out,[10] there have been two themes in this reflection. One is that marriage is about hope for the future. To enter into a marriage is to affirm that God is not yet finished with creation and that it is worth extending the church into the future in anticipation of the coming reign of God. The second theme is that marriage is not first of all about love in the sense that we talk about love in a consumer-capitalist society, but rather about a context within which we practice the virtue of lifelong commitments that help us resist the very consumerist notions that cloud our view of marriage in the first place. Capitalism has always been uncomfortable with long-term commitments and traditions and has become even more so as it has become more oriented to consumption than to production.

Part of the appeal of the notion of romantic love leading to marriage (which now is entered into only after a trial period of "living together" and may be exited as necessary) is that it makes for such efficient consumers. It is not just that weddings have become orgies of consumption, but that the orientation of family life at present is to create new consumers who will arrive at adulthood fully formed in the habits of representing themselves through "consumer choices."[11] In this context, for a preacher at a wedding to speak of "Christian marriage" is ludicrous.

Yet silence is not an option. We are called to preach, to be ministers of the gospel in season and out of season and to extend the church's reflection on the meaning of marriage as a Christian vocation. There are issues that become intertwined in marriage that demand specifically theological reflection. Marriage is one of those boundary places where our vocation in the midst of the ordinary opens transcendent questions. Within a "theology of marriage" that focuses on affirming the ordinariness of our lives in creation, we must also consider what the gospel has to say at this boundary. What we would like to do here, then, is to make some suggestions about how a preacher of the gospel might proceed in preaching at a wedding. We do not believe that what follows is a complete solution to the conundrum of the wedding sermon, but we hope that it might provide a starting point for you the reader to develop your own theology and practice of preaching at weddings.

Discerning the Situation

Weddings, of course, come in all sizes, but one sermon will not fit all. Any of us who has presided at even a few weddings in the past decade or two knows this much. In our limited experience (seminary professors don't get asked to do a lot of weddings), we have presided over first marriages of people who have lived together before getting married, weddings in which one or both of the parties is being remarried after one or more divorces, and weddings in which one or more of the parties is being remarried after the death of a spouse—and mixtures of the latter two. Bob, who began his ministry in Southern California in 1972, cannot remember presiding over any wedding in which the couple was not already living together in some form, so the "traditional wedding" of the 1950s and early '60s would be the one sort of wedding we have not done.

Each and every one of these situations is unique and requires a different approach to the sermon. Theologically the most difficult of these situations should be the remarriage of divorced persons, since that is the one wedding that receives the most negative appraisal in Scripture, but in the contemporary Protestant churches of North America this is no longer the case. For a variety of reasons—some good and some not so good—we have made our peace with divorce and remarriage. Each of the situations that pastors are likely to encounter today raises a variety of theological/pastoral issues that will need to be addressed from the perspective of the value of ordinary life, openness to the future of creation, and the social significance of long-term commitments. Obviously, the first place to address these is in a series of premarital counseling sessions. That is the place where the wedding sermon begins, in the encounter of pastor and couple talking about what is important to each person. This is the primary locus in which the pastor discerns the unique situation of this couple and begins to think through how best to connect them and their marriage to the God who created them and calls them to a vocation of stewardship in the cosmos. We offer these commonplaces—and, given the Lutheran theology of marriage, we are quite intentionally here stretching the concept of "gospel commonplaces"—as helps to your own pastoral and homiletical thought.

Gospel Commonplaces for Wedding Sermons

Commonplace One:
Marriage shows us that God affirms the ordinary and preserves the future of creation.

This may sound a bit radical, and it runs counter to what both of us have thought and practiced for most of our ministries, but if Luther is correct about the centrality of the ordinary life of production and reproduction, there may be no need for us to "Christianize" marriage and certainly no need to sacramentalize it. It has always been the case that the culture of which we are a part has set the standard for what marriage is, how people enter into it, and how it is made public and legal. In medieval Europe the church certainly had some influence on the culture's views on marriage, but—again, if Luther is correct—that may have been a theological mistake. Since marriage is an office of ordinary life in creation, ordinary people practicing marriage in a social community set the parameters of the institution. This is not to say that the disciple community[12] has no interest in the marriages of disciples or the state of relationships in society; it is to say that the church has always followed the lead of culture in deciding who can be married, who is married, and how they make public witness to their marriage.[13]

More importantly, as we secular people practice marriage, we are participating in one means by which God is preserving creation in anticipation of the eschatological fulfillment of the reign of God. In Lutheran theology we have spoken of this traditionally under the rubric of the proper distinction of two kingdoms. Certainly our history shows how horribly this distinction can be abused, but in avoiding the abuse we do need to remember that there is within the distinction of two kingdoms an affirmation of the life that we live in the world. This is not to say that marriage is not a place of moral concern for Christians; it is to say that the moral space within which we discuss marriage is accessible to all, whether Christian or not. The Christian affirmation is that through our daily, ordinary activities in society, we are part of the means by which God preserves and enhances creation. Marriage is one way in which God's "left-handed" work (as it is often called) proceeds. Marriage is a way in which even the most irreligious among us show God's and creation's openness to the future as a new generation comes forth to take up its mission.

> **Implication**—The wedding sermon is not so much a proclamation of the gospel as it is a connection of God's creation through the structures of ordinary social life to this particular couple.

Neither of us can believe that we are saying this, since we both argued for many years that wedding sermons are no different than any other sermon as an explicit proclamation of the gospel of God's grace in Christ. After studying the theology of marriage in developing study materials for the Evangelical Lutheran Church in Canada and in preparing this book, we have changed our minds. Marriage is about creation and God's preserving of creation through human structures. Most of the time when we perform weddings, we do not act as ministers of the gospel but as agents of God's creating and preserving love that has opened the possibility of life in this world to all creatures. When we perform weddings, we act, under the authority of the state, as agents of God's left hand. The wedding sermon is not an evangelistic opportunity in the sense that we are there to convert people; it is an "evangelistic" opportunity in that we are there to call people to a vision of God's deep concern for and involvement in ordinariness. The wedding sermon is an opportunity to focus people's vision away from the starry heavens of romance and toward the divine possibilities of everyday drudgery in the here and now.

There are certainly exceptions to this general rule. In some cases a definite word of gospel is both necessary and appropriate. In these cases properly distinguishing law and gospel means the preacher will discern the situation and apply the word that needs to be heard. In the wedding of two people who have heard the gospel promise for them, the preacher can also affirm that it is God's grace that gives meaning to ordinary life.

> **Implication**—The argument over "sacred" and "secular" in planning wedding services is unnecessary and counterproductive.

The intent is not to separate creation from redemption, but to extend the implications of a specifically Christian and trinitarian doctrine of creation. Both creating the universe and redeeming it are God's work through the Word by the Spirit and express God's grace toward everything that God has created and redeemed. Dividing between some aspects of life that are "sacred" and some that are "secular" is a false distinction. For example, music is music, a gift of God to enable humans to express and experience the full range of being human. Just because a piece of music was originally written to be performed in a church building does not make it somehow more "sacred" than a piece of music written to be performed in a tavern. For pastors and church musicians to argue with a couple over which music is "sacred" is not only silly, but bad theology, too. The same can be said for restricting weddings to church buildings. If marriage is an estate of God's creation, why not hold the wedding in some part of creation that is especially meaningful to the couple?

> ### Commonplace Two:
> *God creates us as a gift for the world and for each other.*

Contemporary theology of creation[14] emphasizes that God's creation of the cosmos is the Trinity's first gift of grace. The Holy One creates the world by the Word through the Spirit so that the love of God for creation is an expression of the love for the other which is at the core of God's being. Just as God's justification of the sinner is an act of pure grace, so creation itself is pure gift. The world and all its creatures are created by grace, preserved by grace, and—having come under the power of sin—saved by grace. While we must make a distinction between fallen nature and grace, the distinction often made between "nature" and grace is a bit misleading. God creates nature as a gracious act, just as God saves fallen nature by a gracious act.

The unique role of humans within creation is to be stewards for others.[15] God placed us within creation to be agents for preservation and nurture, for participation in moving creation from its original goodness toward the potential that God built into the cosmos. The fact that we renounced this vocation in favor of control and dominance—thus necessitating God's intervention in Christ—does not negate the graciousness of the original vocation. We were intended to be God's gifts of grace to the whole of creation. In Christ this vocation that we renounced becomes a new possibility by the action of the Holy Spirit in and through the disciple community.

This means that even today each one of us comes into being by God's grace; our personal creation is a gift as much as the original creation was a gift. Each of us is created to be a gift to the world, a gift to each other, a gift to ourselves. We are created to be persons for others. One way in which we symbolize and actualize this "gift nature" is by opening the totality of our lives to one concrete other. This is not the same as the notions of romantic consumerism in which we select someone who mirrors our own expectations and services our needs—until they no longer do so and then we move on. Obviously, in our culture marriage involves some level of attraction to one another, but from a sense of attraction and shared values and hopes we open ourselves to a lifelong commitment that symbolizes God's relationship to creation (e.g., the New Testament image of the church as bride) and is a specific instance of concretely being persons for others.

This is true no matter how religious or how irreligious or antireligious the people being married might be. God uses human institutions and relationships to preserve creation. Our being aware or unaware of God's working through the structures of the world is not the deciding factor. That being said, it is highly unlikely that most couples—whether raised in the church or not—will come to the pastor with a clear awareness of the import of their marriage for the doctrine of creation and preservation. There will need to be some theological education and the nature and form of that, as well as its expression in the wedding sermon, will need to be shaped by the pastor's discerning of the reality of the couple and their situation. It will certainly be expressed differently for a young couple who have never been married before than it will for two seniors remarrying after the deaths of their spouses.

Implication— "Traditional" marriage is not the only possible form of being for the world and for each other.

As stated earlier, the work that has gone into this chapter began as we participated in preparing a series of study papers for our church as it considered the question of same-sex marriage. Is it possible for a same-sex marriage to be a marriage in the sense that we have been using the word? No one, we think, could dispute that a gay or lesbian couple could symbolize God's faithful commitment to creation. There are just too many instances of same-sex couples who have been faithfully committed to each other for fifty or sixty years to claim otherwise. The depth of these relationships, even during the years when they had to remain hidden, is a reminder of the love of the Creator for creation. Same-sex relationships also affirm the central importance of ordinary life in society. The question is around openness to the future of creation. Since faithful same-sex relationships seem on a biological basis to exclude children apart from extraordinary intervention, one might question whether a same-sex relationship can symbolize openness to the future in the same way that a heterosexual marriage does. In our opinion, the ability to have children apart from medical or other intervention is not at the core of the question. Given the variety and the needs of God's creation, there are a myriad of ways to be open to the future of God's creation that are fully open to all without any regard for the question of sexual orientation.

We need to remember that singleness is also a Christian vocation, one actually recommended by the apostle Paul. To choose or be chosen for the vocation of singleness does not cut one off from the sort of hope for the future that marriage also represents. The single person may well be open to the future in a different way than the married person—though not necessarily so—but the fundamental orientation is the same. Paul's own life can provide a paradigmatic example of singleness for the sake of the future, in his case the future of Gentiles in the Christian community. One also thinks of Dietrich Bonhoeffer in conspiracy and prison for the sake of the future of Germany, Europe, and the church. In the midst of World War II, he became engaged, but both his singleness and his engagement were equally signs of hope. In preaching a wedding sermon, we must never leave the impression that singleness is somehow a second-class vocation, just a different vocation through which we can express hope for God's future.

In the wedding sermon or in premarital counseling, we do want to affirm that the very act of marrying—which certainly no one is required to do today even to enjoy the legal benefits of marriage—is in and of itself an act of affirming the future. By marrying we show that we believe that human institutions are an important part of God's divine providence. We demonstrate our hope that the world will not come to naught, and we join in God's great project of preservation that has come down through the generations. Some of our marriages will be able to include the next generation as our own biological children, some of us will adopt children or nurture foster children so that they might participate more fully in society, some of us will contribute to the welfare of children by being teachers or social workers or community organizers or grocers—or even pastors—and our marriages will be an important part of any vocation to which God calls us. Any one of us and any marriage can be open to the future of creation in a variety of ways.

> **Implication**—Since marriage mirrors God's relationship to creation, wedding sermons recognize that marriage is about reconciling distinct identities.

Part of the doctrine of creation is the affirmation that God and creation are "other" to one another. The Christian doctrine of *creatio ex nihilo* is not pantheism or even panentheism. God created as an act of will—the Christian tradition would want to say gracious, loving will—in freedom. That which is created is separate from and capable of face-to-face relationship with God. The otherness of God and creation to one another is built into the nature of the Creator-creature relationship. The eschatological fulfillment that we hope for is not the merging of creaturely being into divine being, but a renewed, loving relationship between two separate entities. If we want to affirm that marriage is one aspect of God's gifting of creation, then marriage, too, participates in this sense of communion and partnership. The two who "become one flesh" remain at the same time "other" to each other. Marriage is not "I become you and you become me," but "You and I who are separate beings become reconciled to one another in community." This is part of what it means to be created as a gift to one another and to the world. Just as God and the cosmos are separate entities in communion, so a marriage is intended to be two unique persons in communion.

> ### Commonplace Three:
> *Created life together is haunted by the tragic. Marriage relationships take place in the context of fall and sin.*

The "otherness" that had originally and, to some extent, still has a positive sense of unity in diversity and diversity in unity, also has, under the shadow of fall and sin, a darker side. One of the great themes of postmodern philosophy has been the other and the almost insurmountable difficulties we have in dealing with otherness.[16] We seem almost inevitably to read "other" as threat. The other soon enough becomes The Other, and we perceive before us either a god or a monster. So many of the tragedies of human existence seem rooted in our inability to reckon with the other, whether near or far.

The *Lutheran Book of Worship*'s wedding service made this reality quite clear: "Because of sin, our age-old rebellion, the gladness of marriage can be overcast and the gift of the family can become a burden."[17] Sin is certainly part of the issue, yet sin is not the only result of the fall. Our lives are as much haunted by the tragic as by sin. This is one thing that the romantic myth leaves out. No one "lives happily ever after." Marriage is not an escape from our family of origin, nor is it an antidote to our other problems. We carry whatever and whoever we are into marriage. Since what we are after the fall is, in Luther's words, "curved in on ourselves," we will think and act in ways that make relationships more difficult to sustain. The point here is not to excuse bad behavior but to confront reality. My spouse is other, and rather than see that as holding innumerable possibilities for creative relationship, I find it troubling and vaguely threatening.

This is true of all creation after the fall. We no longer have access to the Edenic paradise and must make do with the thorns, thistles, and pain that mark human life in this age. That means that it is not only the romantic myths of consumer capitalism that we must confront, but our own tendencies to overpromise the joys of wedded bliss. We must speak of God's intentions for creation under the proviso that we have taken some initiative and it has not turned out well. None of us is free to construct the perfect marriage; we are all called to explore the possibilities of committed relationship in the midst of a real world that is shaped by both sin and tragedy.

When we speak of marriage as a vocation of God's left hand in the world, we always do so in recognition that life in the world is life lived under the shadow of sin and tragedy. For us humans we live with the results of rejecting our vocation as stewards of God's creation and trying to become creation's lords and masters. We wanted to be the ones to make the decisions, and so now we must. It seems that our choices are always between a bad result and a somewhat less bad result. Praise God it does not happen to very many of us, but every marriage is lived in the knowledge that someday one spouse may have to give doctors the order that ends the machine-supported life of the other. No one seeks such a moment, no one survives such a moment unscarred, but it could come to any of us.

In thinking about Greek and Elizabethan tragedies, we see one aspect of tragedy as the result of trying to manage our moral world. Oedipus's parents try to make sure that the curse can never come true, but the very actions they take to manage the curse make its fulfillment inevitable. Hamlet wants to secure justice for his father, but his actions only lead to an orgy of death and destruction. In our lives we face the temptation of the possibility of the perfect marriage, the partner who will fulfill all our hopes, the ideal children. We try to manage our world, which only makes the odds of tragedy that much better. The preacher at a wedding faces the temptation to try to manage the moral world of the couple by giving advice or finding the perfect sermon that will create a particular atmosphere for the marriage, which does nothing to lessen the hold of sin on human life.

Obviously, this way of understanding the reality of the tragic and sin is specifically Christian theology, not science or cultural wisdom. The word of the cross is not a word that tries to bypass tragedy or even to manage it. The crucifixion of Jesus of Nazareth is what allows us to say in a positive sense that control is beyond us. Here is where one may have to be explicitly evangelistic, that is, make specific reference to the gospel and engage in the art of properly distinguishing law and gospel. What we do in the face of sinful decisions or tragic circumstances is not some form of cultural niceness. We face the ultimate tragedy, the death of God, head-on and proclaim that the God who is revealed in the crucifixion of Jesus of Nazareth has eternally entered into solidarity with all victims of sin and tragedy. We also proclaim our faith and hope that crucifixion is not the end of the story, that resurrection is promised. Yet even resurrection has a cruciform shape: what Thomas wants to see and is invited to touch are the wounds of Jesus. The resurrection is always the resurrection of the *crucified* Jesus and nothing else.[18] There is really no other way to say this than to preach the gospel, so here is where gospel proclamation enters into wedding sermons.

Implication—Beware of the trap of romanticism.

The only message of hope we have to offer people is a hope based in the gospel, the hope of the resurrection of the crucified Jesus. This is not a romantic hope that lusts for living "happily ever after." The ordinary is not a cleaned-up, Disneyfied main street, but the real, dirty, gritty street of joys and sorrows. The Christian preacher is not an apostle of the power of positive thinking or a dispenser of rose-colored glasses even when functioning as an agent of the state or province. The word of God is a word about real life.

Implication—Don't overdo the tragedy.

Being realistic does not mean that Christian preachers live in clouds of doom and gloom either. Our hope is based on the resurrection of the crucified Jesus. God intends for life to be lived to the fullest, for weddings to be joyous celebrations. It was Jesus himself who provided gallons of good wine to keep the party going. People who live in hope are free to love life in ways that people who try hard to believe in positive thinking will never know.

This chapter has taken us on quite a journey. When we set out to write it, we thought that we would say something very different than what we have in fact said. Here are the conclusions we have come to: wedding sermons are about God's goodness in creation and God's "left-handed" methods for preserving creation. Trying to make a wedding "sacred" rather than "secular" is in effect saying "No!" to God's way of being in and for the world as its creator and preserver. In presiding and preaching at weddings clergy are functioning in the realm of the institutions that God has blessed to preserve creation for all creatures. Don't try to make it "Christian," but celebrate the opportunities to be an instrument of God's creative love for everyone.

CHAPTER 5

PREACHING GOSPEL AND STEWARDSHIP

One of the most popular topics either of us is asked to speak or preach on is stewardship. It seems that pretty much every congregation is short of money—a little or a lot—and even if the day-to-day finances of a congregation aren't too bad at the moment, there are a variety of special needs that require more money than is in the treasury. So people want us to come and talk to them about stewardship or they want us to teach them how to talk about stewardship. This need is hardly new. Bob took a course in seminary in 1969 about stewardship programming, and the needs of the average congregation even then required more money than most of them had. Certainly now most congregations are in a deeper financial crisis than they were thirty or forty years ago, and most denominations have far fewer resources than they did then, but what is really different is the cultural context within which we have to talk about stewardship. When Bob entered parish ministry in 1972, the leadership of the congregation was still primarily people who had grown up during the Depression and had come of age during World War II. Those people are now in their eighties or gone altogether. The culture of consumer capitalism, which had certainly gained much strength by the 1970s, has now swept everything else aside, and the sense of civic duty that maintained so many church activities (along with most of the rest of civic society) has waned significantly. People seem to come to church primarily to be "fed" and entertained, not to give and participate. In such a climate, how does one speak meaningfully about stewardship?

Discerning the Context

The context for stewardship preaching in North America today can be summed up in two words: consumer capitalism. It is commonplace to say that we live in a consumer society. When we apply that thought to the church, we often think first about things such as "entertainment evangelism" or "seeker-friendly churches" or similar phenomena. We might not think so deeply about the impact that being formed by consumer capitalism has on how people think about or practice their vocation as stewards of the mysteries of God's grace. The purpose of this section is to introduce some possibilities for that thought. In doing so we will use the terms *consumer capitalism* and *consumerism* interchangeably, but by either of these we mean an economic ideology of free-market capitalism marked by a focus on consumption rather than production. Obviously, production and consumption are intertwined, but one or the other can be seen as the leading factor, and "consumerism" focuses on consumption as the leading factor and consumers as the leading actors.

To have some understanding of the context provided by consumerism, it helps to see that North American capitalism has not always been consumerist. Until the beginning of the twentieth century, production was seen as the leading factor and producers as the leading actors in the economy. Partially this was because the technology of production was such that, under normal circumstances, there was more demand than could be filled. Occasionally there would be a period when demand dropped, times usually referred to as "panics."

It was during this era that the historic "Protestant work ethic" reigned supreme. Beginning with Reformation theologies of vocation as articulated by Luther and Calvin and refracted through Puritans in the United Kingdom and British colonies in North America, the Protestant work ethic taught people that they could become a success in life though hard work and a virtuous character. In the nineteenth century, the commercial and clerical descendants of the Puritans taught Americans and Canadians through tracts and novels that virtues such as frugality, honesty, and reliability and a strong work ethic would lead to success in this world and bliss in the next. In the context of a "new" land where natural resources and opportunity seemed limitless, people lived out these lessons and believed them even in the face of contradictory evidence.[1]

With the invention of the assembly line by Henry Ford in order to produce Model Ts quickly and cheaply, production could exceed demand. This began a shift away from the historic focus on production and producers. New visions of success based on "mind power" and a "winning personality" began to supplant calls for virtue and hard work. The resistance to this trend evaporated in the wake of the Great Depression, when it became clear what the long-term results might be of allowing the new technologies to operate without a parallel change in mind-set. World War II took care of excess production from the late 1930s to the late '40s, but then the stage was set for the full blossoming of consumerism.

Thomas Frank has shown how the needs of corporations drove much of what we are used to thinking of as "the counterculture" of the 1960s in his book *Conquest of Cool*,[2] a survey of advertising and the menswear industries. There he shows that part of what drove the corporate embrace of the counterculture was not just co-option, but a desire on the part of business leaders to convince people to change their outlook on spending and consuming. Frugality was no longer a virtue, but a vice that stood in the way of economic prosperity. Bank loan officers changed from stern enforcers of financial discipline to marketers of product lines through which a person could get access to money to spend on whatever he or she wanted at the moment.

Old attitudes hung on, of course, but they were pretty well eliminated by the time of the rise of neoconservatism in the 1980s. With the world of Ronald Reagan and Margaret Thatcher, the old Protestant work ethic was used only at election time or as a weapon against an imaginary poor who sucked up tax money while adding nothing productive to society, never as something that the middle class was expected to practice.[3] Now there is almost nothing of any ideological power that stands in the way of the "logic of the market" as understood from a consumerist perspective.

The results of this are summarized by Thomas de Zengotita in his recent book *Mediated*.[4] The modern consumer is someone who is always at the center of the media show. Whether watching a commercial or the news, the medium is trying to keep the consumer's attention, to evoke the consumer's desire for more of what is currently on offer. In de Zengotita's formulation, the consumer is constantly being flattered by what is being represented. It is as if everything is *for* the consumer, who sits at the center of a personalized universe. Yet this is an unstable self-centeredness, for we must always be representing ourselves to others in the same way that the media represents the world to us. As a result most of us spend much of our time performing a representation of ourselves, a sophisticated, almost self-parody that we think will gain us some goal that we seek. Even as we play the role for others, they remain instruments for us.

Note that this development is not the product of creeping liberalism or secular humanism. It is the inevitable outcome of the evolution of capitalism. That means that even conservative Christian figures who support capitalism, no matter how conservative their moral pronouncements, are contributing to the change. In fact, what megachurches and conservative Christian organizations must do in order to attract the attention of mediated consumers exacerbates the changes. Even media campaigns against abortion and gay rights—because of the nature of what must be done in order to be noticed—undermine the very "family-centered" values that the Christian Right claims to uphold.

The results of all this have been a disaster for stewardship in churches. Whatever its faults, the old Protestant work ethic contained within it a heavy component of stewardship as one's duty to God and neighbor. As long as that was the cultural norm, most people did their duty and gave time and money to the church as they were able. Not only churches, but most organizations of civil society flourished as people worked together to do what was thought to be best for the communities where they lived. At the same time, church people gave significant amounts of money to the work of denominations and judicatories.

In *Bowling Alone* Robert Putnam records the decline of almost all civil society organizations as consumerism has gained sway in the United States. The membership of most of these organizations is virtually identical: rising through the 1940s and '50s, reaching a peak in the '60s, declining in the '70s and early '80s, and falling off a cliff in the late '80s and '90s. Putnam also breaks down the general statistics to show that the recent decline is not a product of everyone joining less, but of each younger generation participating less than its parents' generation.[5] One possible conclusion is that the more a person has been shaped by the culture of consumerism, the less likely that person is to have any sense of a vocation of stewardship.

This is not to say that the duty of stewardship as understood by the Protestant work ethic is theologically superior to the understanding of the modern consumption ethic. Neither is really based on an understanding of the gospel as God's unconditional grace. At the same time it is clear that the older understanding meant that churches had more members, more participation, and more money. As a result, the shift away from the older sense of producer's duty to the newer sense of consumer's entitlement has led to crisis and panic in many congregations and denominations. Even in those denominations where money and participation are not a crisis, no matter how conservative or liberal, that money and participation must be secured in very different ways than they were even thirty or forty years ago.

Discerning the Situation

The first item we should discuss under this category is whether we should use the word *stewardship*. Many people, quite legitimately, have questioned whether the word has been so corrupted that it cannot be recovered for gospel preaching. In most people's minds, the argument goes, the word is so intertwined with fund-raising that even if it could be recovered, the effort expended could be put to better use. This argument could be correct. The problem is whether another word could convey other necessary connotations of stewardship. In this chapter we will use the word *stewardship*, but we do not intend to imply that this is the only permissible word. We ourselves are in the midst of reflecting whether some other word might well be better. Some that we have tried in the past we have rejected, words such as *management*, which carry with them connotations of corporate authority structures. We encourage you the reader to think about this issue and go beyond what we suggest here.

At least four situations in which one might consider preaching a stewardship sermon present themselves. The first is on those Sundays when the lectionary texts for the week have a stewardship theme or point. On those occasions simply preaching an exegetical sermon on the text or texts will necessarily involve including stewardship themes. This may well be the ideal "situation" for preaching stewardship since it normalizes stewardship preaching. This communicates that stewardship involves a whole set of lifestyle and discipleship issues and is not just a "How do we pay the bills?" issue.

The second potential situation for a stewardship sermon is as part of the annual stewardship campaign or a special emphasis (such as preparing for a building program).

The third situation that might give rise to a stewardship sermon is the existence of an acute or chronic problem with either funding or volunteer involvement in the life of the congregation. In such a case the preacher will want to prepare for a stewardship sermon with a careful analysis of the situation of the congregation. Is the crisis caused because the congregation has gotten a bit stingy or because some significant contributors of money or time have died or become shut in? Is the congregation spending beyond its means, or is it not supplying sufficient means for necessary spending? Has the congregation declined in membership, and thus is in need of new resources to carry out its mission? Has the growth of the congregation necessitated spending or activity at a level the congregation is not used to supporting? Have changes in the neighborhood meant that newer members have less money or time than previous members? These are all questions that need to be asked so that the preacher has some sense of what needs to be addressed.

The fourth situation in which the preacher might consider a stewardship sermon is a bit different. This is the occasion when the focus is on a stewardship issue in the wider community or world. For example, one might preach a sermon on stewardship of the environment on the Sunday after a major report on global climate change is issued. Or one might consider a stewardship sermon when taxes have become a political campaign issue. In these cases the sermon will be a bit different than in the previous three situations, but the basic principles—with reference to some of the *loci* in the chapter on prophetic preaching—will be the same.

Gospel Commonplaces for Stewardship Sermons

Commonplace One:
Stewardship is a way of life.

Most often congregations become interested in stewardship when there is a financial crisis. Perhaps it takes a crisis to focus our attention, but this habit of churches has led us to some false views of what stewardship is really all about. Stewardship is not fund-raising; it is a way of life. A good steward is one who recognizes life as a gift from God and lives life as an offering to God. Certainly, if all of us were living a stewardship lifestyle, no congregation would have financial problems, but fund-raising is not the center of any Christian stewardship program and should not be the primary orientation of any stewardship sermon. The point of preaching stewardship is that people begin to live as servants who nurture God's creation and grace. Stewardship is a way of life in which the followers of Jesus Christ use all that God has placed in their care for the advancement of the mission of God in the world.

"Stewardship" is another way of saying "discipleship." Nurturing the life of stewardship is a central aspect of the ministry of any Christian congregation, because nurturing stewardship is nurturing the life of following of Jesus. It is valuable to talk about "stewardship" as well as "discipleship," because in a consumer society a crucial aspect of discipleship is how we relate to creation. Often we perceive creation as possessions or resources rather than as a gift of God's grace. When we understand ourselves as stewards of God's creation and grace, we challenge that view.

> **Implication**—Stewardship preaching is not a once-a-year activity but should form a part of the total program of the congregation throughout the year.

Any particular stewardship sermon forms a part of a total program of stewardship education in the congregation. Such sermons should support a variety of efforts to help the people of the congregation see the myriad of implications for followers of Jesus in caring for the well-being of the earth and the welfare of the human community. Stewardship sermons are appropriate, for example, around the time of Earth Day when a sermon might focus on the role of Christian people in efforts to apply stewardship to environmental issues.

But even such occasions do not comprehend the universality of the call to stewardship in a Christian's life. Since almost every action we take in the world in our daily lives involves a stewardship decision, almost every sermon should at least take account of the stewardship implications of the text or theme of the sermon. This need goes even beyond the week-by-week ministry of preaching to infuse every aspect of every ministry of the congregation. Stewardship preaching, to be effective, must be part of a wider vision for stewardship and programmatic efforts to open people to God's call to us to participate in the preservation and enhancement of creation.

Implication—While a particular stewardship sermon might focus only on one aspect of stewardship, it should always be a part of a total program to teach and model the whole stewardship lifestyle.

Obviously, a sermon must have a focus and no sermon can be about everything. Yet no sermon in a congregation stands alone. Every particular sermon is a piece of a puzzle with fifty-two or more pieces and takes its place as part of the whole picture that the puzzle presents. This is especially true of stewardship sermons. The temptation is to make the annual stewardship sermon or a sermon in the midst of a financial crisis stand in for the whole program. This is impossible. The sermon has meaning in context, as one part of a whole. The goal is to create a culture of stewardship in a congregation, and in reaching this goal each and every stewardship sermon (and each stewardship Bible study, each stewardship newsletter article, etc.) has its place. Then, when the crisis comes—as it will—a sermon preached in the midst of that crisis will have a foundation to hold it up, a foundation on which the preacher can build.

The same is true of sermons preached as part of a congregation's annual appeal. For the sermon to communicate as fully as possible, that sermon cannot stand alone. It takes its place as one piece of a whole series of events and activities related to communicating the needs of the congregation's mission to members and asking for their support for that mission. As well, the entire annual appeal effort has meaning only in context, as one small piece of the congregation's life.

Implication—In any stewardship sermon the total educational process is more important than immediate fund-raising needs.

Of course, a congregation must have an annual appeal and various special appeals so that there can be enough money to carry out the congregation's mission. At these times the preacher will of necessity speak of God's call on "our" money (see below). The preacher should also remember that even these particular sermons are part of a whole, and that whole has long-term implications that are more important than next year's budget or a necessary building project.

Since we have both been parish pastors and are now members of a congregation, a synod, and a seminary with financial issues, we know just how pressing these needs can be. Even in the worst financial crises, we must remind ourselves to look at the whole picture of mission and stewardship and not get caught up in the atmosphere of crisis.

The truth is that too often our churches face these situations, not because the members do not have enough money for their own needs, but because they confuse consumer desire with actual need and divert money that could well be used for mission. The root of our financial crisis is in a deeper crisis of unbelief in the church—too many of us simply do not believe the gospel to be true. We worship a stingy god in the midst of a stingy society, and so we are stingy in our giving. This is a situation that did not begin yesterday and will not be solved tomorrow by manipulating people to give a bit more money today.

It is also a situation that can be masked in congregations that are outwardly successful. Just because a congregation has no money worries and/or is growing in membership, we cannot assume that a culture of stewardship prevails in that congregation. The stewardship crisis runs deeply in our whole culture (have you seen the film *An Inconvenient Truth*, featuring Al Gore?). As long as we live in a society that has been shaped by the ethos of consumer capitalism, stewardship will be one of our most serious issues, especially among those who have plenty of money to spend and whose institutions are growing. Successful congregations need to learn stewardship and need to hear stewardship sermons.

Commonplace Two:
Stewardship is nurturing what the Creator has made.

God is the creator of the whole world and is the loving redeemer of all creation. When we confess the Apostles' Creed, we confess in the first article that God is the creator of all things. In the second article we confess our faith that God the Creator is also at work in Jesus Christ redeeming the whole of creation. In the third article we confess that God the Holy Spirit is at work today moving creation toward the ultimate resurrection. Stewardship is about all of this, about the care and nurture of all that God has made and all that God is redeeming. Stewardship is about God's creation and God's redemption, and it is about God calling us to join in this trinitarian project.

In the ancient world and the Middle Ages, a "steward" was a manager of someone else's property. Since God is the creator and redeemer of everything that exists, everything belongs to God. Stewardship involves the use we make of all that God has originated and all that God will bring to fulfillment. Those things that we call "ours" (our bodies, our minds, our souls, our abilities, our homes, our families, our jobs, our income, our city, our environment—everything) all belong to God. God has lovingly entrusted these things to us so that we can participate in God's mission in the world; that is, so that we can be part of God's work of saving the world God created. Everything we have is a gift from God; nothing is our own property. Everything we have is given to us so that we can be a part of God's mission. The point of any stewardship sermon is to teach us how to care for and enhance whatever God entrusts to our care.

Implication—A stewardship sermon should challenge our cultural definition of "ownership" and teach Christians to see all of their personal "possessions" and the whole world as belonging to God.

This may well be the hardest part of preaching a stewardship sermon. It is bad enough for the church to be "always asking for money," but it is an irritant of a whole other order for the church to suggest that my money isn't really mine at all. At least since John Locke suggested that it was human labor that turned raw (and relatively valueless) nature into property, modern citizens of Europe and North America have assumed that private property is sacred and it is *mine* because I *worked* for it. In such a culture, notions of grace and the world as a good gift become almost impossible.

The life of a gospel preacher who points this out will not necessarily be easy, yet there does not really seem to be much choice. The gospel just *is* the message of radical grace. We have not earned one iota of what we use. The law simply does reveal our pretensions of ownership for what they are, a product of original sin. The Bible is quite clear about God's economics—much clearer than it is about God's views on sex. It is not pleasant to hear that our consumer, capitalist way of life systemically violates God's law day in and day out. Yet what can we say? That God actually approves of our looting and pillaging the earth and then taking the proceeds as our own? That God wants us to keep the poor in poverty?

If you reacted to that last bit when you read it the way we did when we wrote it, you are now either furious or drowning in guilt and shame. Either response is equally unhelpful. Stewardship preaching is not about making people mad—though truthful stewardship preaching probably will make some people mad—nor is it about making people feel guilty—though encounters with the law have always had a habit of doing that. Truthful stewardship preaching is about challenging all of us to hear God's word here and now, especially as that word speaks to our culture's conceits. Preachers will want to present the message as winsomely as possible, but there remains an unalterable challenge in Scripture to modern notions of ownership. Stewardship is about who owns what.

Commonplace Three:
Stewardship is God's mission.

The reason for the church's being is mission. This focus is not some self-chosen work or institutional advancement; the mission is always and only the mission of God. The mission of God is to bring about the reign of God, to move creation toward the perfection that God intended from the beginning. When our human attempt to become self-creators bent creation away from God's purposes, God intervened and sent Jesus to redirect creation along its original trajectory. Thus, the mission of God involves both the preservation of creation and the salvation of the world in Christ. Christian stewards have been made participants in this mission by the work of the Holy Spirit through word and sacrament. Thus, the call to a lifestyle of stewardship is a call to a life that uses resources to care for creation, to make peace, to increase justice, and to proclaim the gospel. The care of creation includes the way we live out our vocation and the lifestyle of our home and family.

> *Implication*—The goal of preaching a stewardship sermon is to make our congregation more effective in our part of God's mission.

This is a corollary of the implication that the total educational goal of stewardship is more important than immediate needs. In any individual sermon, the mission of God in and for creation is the overarching concern. At the same time, there is a particular and contextual goal: this particular community can become a more effective part of God's mission, so a sermon can and should be very specific in helping people see possibilities for their own and their community's stewardship living.

> *Implication*—A stewardship sermon should present a vision for the mission of God through the congregation.

Communities of Christians are doubly responsible for stewardship. Like every other human community, we are stewards of God's creation who are called to leave the earth a more fruitful place than we found it. Christian communities have a second, more unique call to be "stewards of the mysteries of God"— stewards of the gospel. That second stewardship, stewardship of redemption, is at the core of why we even have communities of Christians. Congregations are called to be in mission, and stewardship preaching is a vital part of nurturing that mission.

Congregational stewardship programs should make it easy for people to find their place as participants in mission. Stewardship programs must involve a public, open, and transparent process of budgeting for the congregation, so that people can see that the whole community has a sense of stewardship and can feel confident that resources are being used appropriately. In addition to budget, there should also be a clear statement of the congregation's vision for mission, goals, and objectives so that the calls for stewardship living can elicit a concrete response.

It is always more effective to present the needs in *mission* terms rather than accounting terms. The parish council should be able to show people that the resources they entrust to the congregation will really be used to make the church a more effective communicator of the gospel in the community. A council might, for example, decide to present a "narrative budget" to the congregation that uses multiple media and presents spending decisions based on what is being accomplished with the money.

The stewardship sermon plays an important role in this process. In preaching, the pastor of the congregation points to a biblical vision for mission that is both local and global. The preacher can articulate a vision for a congregation in ways that are simply not available to other leaders in the community, so the vision presented should be as comprehensive and holistic as possible. At the same time, people respond to a vision much more readily when they see ways in which they can take concrete actions in their own context. The preacher walks a line where balance includes both the visionary and the concrete.

Implication—A congregational stewardship program includes helping Christian people deal with the vocational and lifestyle issues of modern life.

This is also part of the wider vision of stewardship as a way of life rather than just fund-raising. Any work that we do in the church to teach stewardship must take into account that we are teaching stewardship *living* in our particular consumerist context. Within this context every follower of Jesus is called to be in mission throughout life. Everything we do every day is part of this mission.

Our context in North America makes this mission all the more difficult. We are constantly being formed as efficient consumers, and the habits of efficient consumption make for poor stewardship and ineffective mission.

Implication—The needs of God's mission in the world should take precedence over the needs of the congregation.

This is a hard one. We want our congregations to do well, and we want to be successful in our vocations. In addition, the media of the consumer society call out to us to put ourselves at the center of concern. When we preach and teach that God's mission takes precedence over our own needs or the immediate needs of our congregation is much like the story told of the eleventh-century king Canute of England commanding the tide not to come in. Yet it is possible to raise our own sights and raise the sights of the people who hear us preach.

Commonplace Four:
Stewardship is gospel.

The point of preaching a stewardship sermon is to motivate people to be stewards, to live in some form a stewardship way of life. Stewardship is the way of life of people who have been captured by the love of God. This love was originally expressed in creation. The vocation of steward was part of that original, gracious creation. Part of the fall is the human decision that being an owner is always better than being a steward. Thus, God's undoing of the fall, God's healing of creation in Christ, involves returning humans to our original vocation. This is good news, a message that is expressed in the gospel of Jesus Christ. The vocation of steward is a gift from God, not a requirement of the law. Therefore, the motivation for stewardship is a motivation of the gospel, not a motivation of the law.

Implication—In motivating people to be good stewards, we should avoid appeals to duty, threat, or reward. While such motivations may produce money, they will never produce stewardship.

When Bob was a parish pastor, he lived in a neighborhood that was often targeted by certain evangelists for money-raising campaigns. One such was the "Reverend" who sent out a quarterly magazine that told the stories of all the people who had joined the evangelist's "Gold Book Plan." To join the plan, you requested a book of coupons and then sent in a coupon and offering every month. In the magazine was story after story of those who had joined the plan and then received something they had been praying for. One received a gift of cash, another a new Cadillac. Some even ended up with new houses! Then there were one or two stories of those who had put off joining the plan until something terrible had happened. Then they had seen the error of their ways and joined up. Now all their problems were solved. The magazine's appeal must have been at least moderately successful, since the magazine came quarter after quarter. The evangelist was never a big name, but he seemed to make a decent income.

Most preachers know that we should neither promise people rewards if they give nor threaten them with punishments if they do not give. We are a bit too sophisticated to be crass legalists just like those we sometimes like to think of as "the evil televangelists." We know, though, that we ourselves and many of the preachers we have heard over the years have made more than a few appeals to people to do their duty and support the ministry of the church with time, talent, and treasure. The duty appeal may not be crass legalism, but it is legalism nonetheless.

Luther is quite clear on this point. Trying to motivate people to live the Christian life (which is really just another way of saying the stewardship way of life) through the law is like trying to get an apple tree to bear fruit by lecturing it. What brings an apple harvest is manure, water, and letting the tree do what God created it to do. *Lex semper accusit* —"the law always accuses." The law cannot by its nature motivate a Christian life. It is powerless. Duty, threat, or reward can never make a person a steward; only the love of God in Christ can make people stewards. Attempts to motivate people by the law may bring in money—maybe even a lot of money—but they cannot enable people to be stewards.

Commonplace Five:
Stewardship involves money.

While fund-raising is not stewardship, the use and giving of money is central to a stewardship lifestyle. This is because money is one of the most potent symbols of our culture. We have learned to measure our worth and value in terms of income. Money determines status and importance in our world. If something (clean air, for example) cannot be expressed in terms of a dollar value, we often fail to recognize its value or even its existence. Because money is so important to us as modern North Americans, it is an important stewardship issue. It is sad but true that the amount of money people provide for the work of the congregation often shows how important the mission of God is for them. While stewardship preaching cannot focus on fund-raising, neither can it avoid serious talk about the use of money.

> **Implication**—The way that the congregation uses the monetary resources it has been given is an important teaching tool.

One of the most important questions to ask when evaluating the stewardship of the congregation as a community is this: "Does our congregation spend most of its money on itself or on others?" The yearly congregational budget should express the same attitude that we want each member to have. The congregational budget will either support what the preacher says from the pulpit or argue against it. While a budget is necessary for administrative and accounting purposes, a congregational budget is first of all an embodiment of the congregation's sense of mission.

> **Implication**—A stewardship sermon needs to address the question of money squarely and honestly.

In one congregation Bob served, he was puzzled by a comment he often heard when calling on people who had visited worship: "I like your church. You only take one offering." Only later did he discover that it was the custom of some churches in that community to take offerings until the amount of money the pastor thought necessary had been contributed. It is a common complaint that the church only wants to talk about money. In our experiences in mainline churches, that complaint doesn't reflect reality. More often in our churches, there seems to be a strong taboo against discussing money—people talk more about sex and death than they do about money!

This is perhaps a taboo that the preacher should consider breaking. By this we do not mean a steady stream of fund-raising sermons, but careful reflection on the role that money plays in our lives. Certainly, Jesus was not afraid to discuss money, and these texts recur in the lectionary. Stewardship emphases also give the preacher the opportunity to talk directly about the power that money wields over us.

> **Implication**—The money that people do not give to the church is as important as the money they do give.

A stewardship sermon should speak to our total use of money. This is the difference between talking honestly about our use of money and incessant fund-raising. Talking about money means talking about our involvement in the consumer society. At some point we must address the problem of "affluenza."[6] Are the members of our congregation spending all of their money in ways that participate in God's mission in the world? Do we spend our money in ways that help or hurt the environment? Do we spend our money in ways that hurt the people of the "two-thirds" world? These are just some of the possible questions that a stewardship sermon might raise about money.

Commonplace Six:
Stewardship is community.

The stewardship lifestyle can only be lived by people together in community, never by "rugged individualists." When Jesus called his disciples, he formed them into a community. As the apostles proclaimed the gospel, they formed communities in each town they visited. Even today, the Holy Spirit gathers people into community through the word and the sacraments. Community and life in a community of word and sacrament is essential to the practice of Christianity and to the practice of stewardship.

The forces of modern life press us away from stewardship toward a life of thoughtless consumption, so we stand in special need of the supportive network of a community of stewards in Christ. There is no such thing as a self-made steward. One movement that understands this well is the Iona Community, based in Scotland. The Iona Community, best known outside the United Kingdom for its contributions to worship and hymnody, is also well known on its home turf for members who are active in working for peace and justice. It is a "dispersed Christian ecumenical community working for peace and social justice, rebuilding of community and the renewal of worship."[7] The members of the community follow a discipline that includes accountability to one another for the use of time and money.[8] This kind of stewardship derives from a community shaped by the message that God's grace is without measure, that God always provides abundance, never scarcity.

The stewardship sermon has an important role to play in forming such a community. The preacher provides hearers with an alternative to the individualistic consumer society by using biblical passages, metaphors, and images that embody the alternative vision of the reign of God. In addition, the stewardship sermon, as part of the liturgy of word and sacrament, enables people to see the link between the language of stewardship and the acting out of community as all gather to share the meal that has been provided in whole by Christ himself. The incredible generosity of Jesus, who gave his body to feed his people in community, is the content of the life of stewardship.

Martin Luther put it well in his 1519 sermon "The Blessed Sacrament of the Holy and True Body of Christ . . .": "In this sacrament, therefore, man is given through the priest a sure sign from God himself that he is thus united with Christ and his saints and has all things in common [with them], that Christ's sufferings and life are his own, together with the lives and sufferings of all the saints."[9]

Implication—It is vitally important that stewardship sermons support the development of community in the congregation.

Any sermon that supports an individualistic spirituality undermines the life of stewardship. In our age this is a difficult reality, since the forces of the culture seem to favor an approach to religion as "that which feels right to me."[10] Many churches have cultivated such a spirituality in order to attract seekers—which is most certainly a worthy goal. The problem is what exactly it is to which people are being attracted. Perhaps it is not the life of stewardship. Even so well known a "seeker-friendly" church as Willow Creek is now having second thoughts about the results of their efforts in forming a community of disciples.[11] Individualistic, "results-oriented" preaching may only reinforce the habits of the consumer society that make stewardship so difficult.

Implication—Serious efforts toward stewardship may require us to look carefully at the structures of our congregational life and evaluate their effectiveness in teaching stewardship and building community.

This follows from the previous implication. Do we as a congregation or parish promote community through our structures and programming? How can we structure and program so as to promote community and thoughtful discipleship? How can our preaching support such programming?

To sum up, the issue is fairly straightforward. Stewardship preaching should not play to the consumerist mind by replicating its form and content. If stewardship preaching is indeed gospel preaching, it should lead us toward a different vision: one focused on the stewards' way of life, the God who has entrusted this world to our care and the way this God has called us into partnership for mission. Such a focus may well call our lives as lived into question. More importantly, however, this stewardship focus will call us into the heart of the gospel.

CHAPTER 6

PREACHING GOSPEL IN THE FACE OF INJUSTICE

W hat do you say when a situation of injustice claims the attention of a congregation? What do we *preach* when the world seems to be overwhelmed by the tears of those who suffer because of the actions of others? Sometimes our churches experience such situations firsthand: a local company declares bankruptcy and people's jobs and pensions are erased just after the CEO garners a huge severance with monster perks; a community learns that a beloved local pastor has been exploiting children sexually over the years while some church members and juridical bodies tried to keep it hushed up; or a town's racist attitudes surface in vigilante attempts to curb illegal immigration in their community. On other occasions, however, such situations of injustice are perceived more from afar yet still manage to have an impact on the church where you are through the media: dour-looking national leaders debating questions of war and peace in far-flung places or pictures of a genocidal melee half a world away splashed across the pages of the local newspaper. Sometimes such events become so big and important, we can't remain silent. While some social-justice preaching will arise naturally out of our study of lectionary texts, there are moments in public life that are so compelling that they require a kind of direct theological address. On days like that, how do we preach the gospel in the face of injustice?

This is a theological question, not just an exegetical question. The examples above are all ones that one could preach on with the help of biblical prophets. In fact, a preacher's first impulse may be to correlate well-known biblical texts with such situations of injustice: Micah's "swords into plowshares" for questions of war and peace, or Amos's "woes to the wealthy" for the exploitative corporate CEO. Yet while such biblical texts are important and helpful, they don't necessarily solve the theological problem we want to probe. How does the gospel that we are called to preach speak contextually to such situations? The question is not just whether the eighth-century prophets had a word from the Lord. This question is, Do *we*?

Preachers trying to do this hard theological work in preaching in the face of social injustice will face several temptations. One theological temptation in such moments will be to turn to the crutch of moralism. In our culture it is easy to confuse preaching with the thundering voice that tells people what to do. On the theological right this tends to sound like this: "If only we had more family values," or "People need to take more personal responsibility." Yet a similar problem shows up on the theological left, too. Here it is tempting to turn every sermon into homiletical salad, with "lettuce" conclusions: "Therefore *let us* be more inclusive" or "*Let us* build the kingdom of justice." In either case, the result is frequently a theologically truncated message that tends toward moralism.[1] Theologian Ed Farley notes that in such instances the cultural trend of moralism tends to displace the theological task and thus usurp the place of the gospel—especially in preaching where it turns the goal of proclamation into offering "lessons of life."[2]

A second temptation is to confuse preaching in such moments with our own righteous indignation—as if our anger alone would be sufficient to persuade. Sometimes we preach as if the old maxim were true: "If you aren't convinced, I'll just say it more loudly." This temptation looms large when our own pulpit presence is suffused with an overly strong identification with the prophets of old. Two assumptions may be at work here. In too many North American pulpits there is too little differentiation between the angry voice of wrath and preaching with passion. African American homiletician Henry Mitchell points out that there's a difference between "fiery mad" and "fiery *glad*."[3] Yet even if this inability to distinguish is not part of the mix, the second assumption is just as pernicious. We tend in our own minds to associate the prophets almost exclusively with the emotion of righteous indignation. Yet, as biblical scholar Walter Brueggemann notes, the prophetic imagination proceeds not so much from anger, but from *grief*.[4] All this is not to say that anger is categorically wrong. In fact, there will be times when it will be important. The point, rather, is that we need to attend more deeply to what it means to preach the gospel in the face of social injustice. If the biblical prophets themselves are more than angry soapbox preachers, perhaps a *theological* view of preaching in situations of injustice can ground our prophetic preaching not just in anger, but in the *passion* of solidarity in shared grief.

Given these temptations, a theology of the gospel may just be the best guide for preaching in the face of injustice. Thus far, we have ventured a somewhat traditional starting point for our homiletical-theological reflection on the gospel: namely, justification by grace through faith. Yet our starting point in the Reformation's key gospel insight on justification also opens up new vistas when applied to moments when preaching addresses situations of social injustice. Since this gospel of justification by grace through faith sets us free from concern with our own salvation, we can articulate how we in Christ are freed to seek the health and welfare of the community. Thus, our goal is not simply to tell people what to do, let alone merely to engage in righteous indignation, but to announce with Luke 4 the good news that God in Christ intends

> "to bring good news to the poor, . . .
> to proclaim release to the captives
>   and recovery of sight to the blind,
> to let the oppressed go free,
> to proclaim the year of the *Lord's* favor."
> (Luke 4:18b-19, emphasis ours)

As hearers of that news, we are not so much obligated as freed to get with God's program for the sake of the world God so loves. In such moments, then, there is an intimate link between preaching the gospel of Christ *and* the gospel Christ himself preached: the good news of the kingdom of God (Mark 1:14-15).

In talking about gospel and public situations of injustice in this way, we open up an important problem for Christian theology: the place of gospel preaching in the public sphere. Some have used the Reformer Luther's distinction between the two kingdoms to justify a kind of Christian quietism. In this quietistic interpretation, the church, under the orders of redemption, has nothing to say to the world under the orders of creation. The distinction, however, may just have a greater value when retrieved in a context of worldly pluralism. The order of redemption lives primarily from the gospel, which frees humanity to "let God be God." In the order of creation, however, which lives under law, the effect of the distinction is to "let the world be the world."[5] Luther's distinction, viewed rightly, therefore allows for a preaching of the gospel that sets the world free to be what the world really is. This both invites the kind of gospel preaching we are promoting and helps us to see its limits. The goal of gospel preaching in the face of injustice is not to Christianize a secular and pluralistic world, but to help the world be what it really is: a place of justice and God's ongoing creative work. In this way, preaching gospel in the face of injustice actually honors Luther's distinction of the two kingdoms.

Yet even this truth about gospel proclamation in the face of injustice remains far too general apart from considerations of context. Therefore, in order to articulate the gospel clearly, we need to begin by understanding in greater detail the contextual features of our common life that interact with our gospel speech. Once there, we can identify some useful gospel commonplaces that will help us fulfill our calling to announce the good news that makes for justice.

Discerning the Context

The Church and the Culture of Therapy

A preaching of the gospel that engages situations of injustice runs up against one barrier in our therapeutically oriented culture. Our culture embodies a general religious tendency toward viewing faith as a matter both personal and private. From the quest for personal spiritualities apart from institutionalized religion in books and retreats all the way to afternoon talk shows like *Oprah* and *Dr. Phil*, North Americans have subsumed the life of faith under a kind of culturally assumed therapeutic introspection. As a result, especially in middle-class churches, it becomes difficult for many to conceive of the religious life apart from the consumerist, religious individualism of what Robert Bellah has called "habits of the heart."[6]

This contextual feature, however, poses both difficulties and offers opportunities to the person committed to preaching the gospel in the face of injustice. The difficulties, of course, have to do with the truncated view of faith that such a cultural view presupposes. The idea that it is possible to be personally religious while the world goes to hell in a handbasket is contrary not only to the gospel, but to the earliest biblical witness as well. In this sense, the focus on the gospel as beginning in God's justifying love is key. It breaks through an inordinate concern for self to the end that we are freed for loving neighbors. Nonetheless, lurking within our middle-class obsession about ourselves is also a longing that may prove helpful for preaching. In the desire to move toward personal wholeness, we may well be able to identify places where human beings can connect new lines of empathy and solidarity with each other. In the face of the cross itself, we Christians experience ourselves as judged. At the cross, our deathly attempts at saving ourselves are revealed for what they are. Yet at the cross we also experience ourselves as steadfastly redeemed. God's unrelenting empathy and solidarity with humanity are revealed in the cross to the uttermost. Precisely in those places where we can *admit* the deformation of our lives as lived in a culture of therapy, we have the opportunity to open ourselves anew. This means relating not only to others who struggle but to the Other who was revealed in sure judgment and unrelenting mercy in the cross.

Church as Sanctuary from Politics

The private shape of religious faith is also evident in the way in which people relate the life of faith to public matters. Although the idea of the wall of separation between church and state has become an important feature of U.S. jurisprudence around the interpretation of the First Amendment of the U.S. Constitution, the idea has some unofficial cultural currency in Canada as well. The popular assumption is that religious affections naturally "affect" people with power, from voters all the way to public officials. The ideal, however, is that religious faith should affect individual persons in an indirect way, that is, not in the rough and tumble of policy and law. The religious realm in this view is a private realm. The public realm, by contrast, is a place where people make arguments according to universal canons of reason and without resort to claims about transcendence. As a result, religious discourse is marginalized and made a matter of private taste and not public good.

Religious persons have a rhetorical burden in dealing with this view of the church as a kind of private sanctuary from the public realm. The church has had a heavy hand historically in how it deals with public matters and has clearly abused its powers. Religious wars throughout the world, crusades, and the wielding of power in missional, colonial contexts bears witness to the church's sin. As the church in North America becomes increasingly disestablished, however, the church as an institution just may have new opportunities for reengaging life in the public square. While it should be duly chastened for its abuses of power, its loss of power in the new context of disestablishment may just open opportunities for it to reengage the culture in a humbler and more cooperative spirit. We say "humbler," because the church is as corrupt as any human institution around it. We say "cooperative," because other religious and nonreligious groups stand ready to join a public dialogue in a post–9/11 world. Yet if we are to do so, we will need to understand our public role with all its risks. In doing so, we will find ourselves entering the pluralistic and public world of what Parker Palmer called "the company of strangers."[7] This means that we will need to articulate a way of doing theology that is intelligible across religious lines and done in a way that allows Christian persons to work cooperatively with strangers: religious and nonreligious alike. Yet in our own traditions, we can still take comfort. True, the stranger is experienced both then and now as threat. Yet in our tradition we know that strangers can also bring blessing, as the three visitors to Abraham and Sarah bear witness (Genesis 18). In fact, in Jesus' vision of the sheep and goats in Matthew 25, strangers even serve as windows to Christ himself.

Prophetic Preaching and the Problem of Civil Religion

One of the greatest difficulties for prophetic preachers is posed by the predominance of American civil religion. As Canadian Americans who have also lived overseas for a time, we both have noticed that Christian churches in many countries outside the United States generally don't feature the presence of national flags in their worship spaces. In the United States, however, it is not only typical, but also expected. There is especially in religious life in the United States a strange confluence of religious and national symbols—and the expectation is that religious life should be a theological extension of national feelings about country, sacrifice, loyalty, and exceptionalism.

To be sure, there are times in American civil religion when the symbols of the state are bent toward gospel purposes. Prophetic preachers remember with gratitude the marvelous fusing of Christian and American symbols in Martin Luther King's "I have a dream" message. There are times, too, when American civil religion also is able to critique itself and not merely be a self-justifying ideology for nationalism and/or industrial interests. Thomas Jefferson said, "I tremble for my country when I remember that God is just." Lincoln, in the midst of the Civil War, could also imagine the strange ways that divine providence was working itself out without recourse to the kind of jingoism that marks so much of civil religion today. Yet these very exceptions should serve as warnings to gospel preachers. The will to power of a nation is as, if not more, dangerous than that of the rapacious individual. Gospel preachers will need to exercise discernment here so that national goals of glory and honor are not confused with a divine will revealed as strangely self-emptying on the cross: a symbol of the merciless pretensions of empire and yet the foolishly weak "power of God" revealed in compassionate mercy.

Church as Economically and Politically Enmeshed Institution

Preaching that desires to speak in situations of injustice cannot do so apart from an awareness of its own complicity in contemporary economic arrangements. After the Enron scandal, it became customary on Canadian TV shows where mutual-fund managers and investment gurus were interviewed to have such guests disclose whether they held any of the investments they discussed in their segment. In some media circles, these investment experts were required to declare possible "conflicts of interest." Perhaps we in the church should get up to speed. For most of us mainliners, clergy participate in a pension program whose value rises or falls with the wider market. In these days, it is also not uncommon that congregations will draw some income either from properties they hold or from investments they benefit from in endowments and other funds. While from time to time churches are moved to divest from situations where there is rank injustice (e.g., South Africa in the 1980s), there is, apart from such moments, little recognition that the church of God has a substantial stake in the god of the marketplace and the working of that god's "invisible hand" for the supposed benefit of buyers and sellers everywhere.[8] Thus, when we preach in the face of injustice, we will need to do so with an acknowledgment of our own enmeshment and without any plausible claim to purity or perfection.

As such, when we engage for justice in the world, we will be doing so coming under the same judgment and mercy of the cross as anyone else. The cross reveals our complicity with stark clarity. The empire, the religious leaders of the day, and even the crowds get in on the crucifixion action. Yet at the cross we also see God's redemptive mercy. On the cross that mercy is shown for what it is: steadfast, unrelenting, a compassionate power revealed in brokenness. We may sometimes think that preaching in situations of injustice is a matter of pointing fingers and thundering voices. After the cross, however, prophetic preaching should sound different. In a community that points to the Risen, *Crucified* One in its weak word of preaching and humble thanksgiving banquet of broken bread and poured-out wine, preaching gospel in such moments should look and sound different. We should know such preaching as born in a solidarity of *shared* judgment; it should live longingly for its revelation of solidarity in shared redemption. Because of its own complicity, it lives not from its own righteousness from on high, but from a grace that grants it provisional signs of resurrection newness. In this way, it is empowered to live ever more justly by helping it to live ever more freely by the mercy of God.

This ecclesial self-awareness speaks to a basic shape of thought by which we might view matters of injustice. Homiletician David Buttrick argues that the structure of our awareness is basically "double-minded": we preach to a community "being-saved-in-the-world."[9] Within the Reformation tradition, there is something of an analogue in one of the basic paradoxes that governed Luther's thinking: that we are *simul justus et peccator*, that is, simultaneously justified and yet sinners.[10] This basic stance or shape of mind does not allow us to view the problem of injustice as one simply "out there." Because of this, the church's stance in situations of injustice can never simply be finger pointing. The *justus* points us toward our own dawning sense of God's justifying mercy in Christ that is not only for me (*pro me*), but for us (*pro nobis*). The fact that we are also at the same time *peccator* is a reminder of our common worldly brokenness. Such a shared sense of our paradoxical reality keeps us honest about ourselves, our churches, our neighbors in the community, and our whole world. Christians have not graduated from humanity; nor has the church as the vanguard of redemption graduated from creation. Ironically, this paradox keeps Christian preaching in the face of situations of injustice *real* about our human brokenness and focused on a divine redemption in the gospel that bears witness in Christ to the world God so loved. Properly conceived, this ecclesial awareness keeps the church humble. Such awareness keeps us in connection with a broader humanity. Ultimately, it helps us live within a divinely justified solidarity with all the ungodly, whether in the church, the community, or the wider world.

Discerning the Situation

A situation that calls for preaching gospel in the face of injustice can take many shapes. We might identify a series of possibilities that we could set within interlocking and encompassing circles:

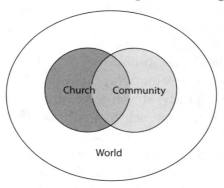

The point here is merely that to be in the church is at once to be in a wider community and the world. When we deal with a situation of injustice in the church, for example, we approach the situation not only in our ecclesial awareness, but within worldly perspectives, too.

Given this reality, it is more helpful to think of situations of injustice that might call for a gospel word as falling along a continuum:

Injustice in Church >>> Injustice in Community >>> Injustice in World

The distinctions here are set along this continuum because they are not discrete. The continuum enables us to identify our perceived proximity to the situation of injustice.

Perceived Proximity to Injustice

With this aspect of the situation, we explore whether the issue of injustice involved touches more or less on the fabric of church life with respect to the life of redemption or whether it is properly an area of concern in light of our more broadly shared status as creatures with all creation. The distinction is not absolute but will prompt different kinds of gospel issues. A problem of injustice in the church will necessarily evoke theological *loci* that speak to the church's life, its dependence on the means of grace in word and sacrament, the fabric of life lived in the Spirit, as well as the cruciform shape of a uniquely Christian discipleship. A problem in the world, especially one where the church is not immediately implicated, will quite possibly more likely touch on matters of creation, providence, (general) revelation, and theological anthropology. In most cases, the *loci* that speak to injustice in the world will be *added* to the *loci* in the church, precisely because of the church's paradoxical relationship with community and in the world. The value of the distinction is not found in a rigid slotting of theological *loci*, but in identifying the different hearers with which the gospel engages in a given (rhetorical) situation. The theological justification for such a move is the incarnation itself. Christ does not become incarnate in the church only, but for the sake of the world God so loves. While, as John the evangelist points out, there is a tragic element in that the world *receives him not*, such rejection does not forestall his incarnation but leads it more profoundly to a "lifting up" in cross and resurrection. Even John's Gospel, for all its dualism, cannot bracket itself from the world. It engages nonetheless in conversation, even in the midst of tragic misunderstanding and rejection, as it points to "exaltation" in the midst of dying and rising as the very telos or "end" of incarnation.

Situations and Context Revisited

In light of these contexts and our perceived proximity to a given situation of injustice, gospel preachers will need to attend to certain realities. In preaching gospel in the face of injustice, preachers need to be aware of the many different sides and interests that attend such preaching. Preachers cannot merely assume that certain *attitudes and ideologies* exist outside the church; to the contrary: they are already here among us. Honest prophetic preaching allows us to face the brokenness that is injustice from within the double-sided nature of our ecclesial self-awareness described above.

Such preaching will also need to confront a pluralism of *pieties and theologies* that exist inside the church. When we turn to the tradition, it cannot be some pure monolith that authorizes a word from on high. In this sense, our preaching gospel in the face of situations of injustice will need to come face-to-face with its own provisionality. For that matter, for the sake of viewing the ministry of gospel preaching within the context of the whole of ministry, we will need to be humble. Although our provisional sense of the gospel as justification by grace through faith impels us to speak, as a mediation of gospel in this time and place, our speaking will also come under the eschatological reservation: for *"now we see through a glass darkly"* (1 Cor. 13:12a KJV). Gospel gives us direction; it may not give us *the answer* for this situation.

In articulating such a direction, we'll discover that such situations also call for a whole ministry approach that includes pastoral engagement in all of life: the prophetic gospel sermon is located and relates to *pastoral care and political engagement in the world*. This is to say that every moment of engagement for others opens up the possibility of a solidarity in difference. Preaching gospel in the face of injustice does not simply speak pure transcendence from on high, because all preaching and life come under the shadow of the cross, where both our profound brokenness *and* connection are revealed.

For that matter, such situations also lift up important features of pastoral leadership. Although preaching gospel in the face of injustice is grounded in pastoral and political relationships marked by solidarity in difference, leadership itself needs to open up to a connection strong enough to sponsor differentiation. In other words, preachers as congregational leaders saying sometimes yes and sometimes no in the church, help make possible a church that can say yes and no to the wider world when situations of injustice pull us out of our ecclesial cocoons into the world God so loves.

Our basic thesis is that preaching gospel in the face of injustice requires having clarity about that gospel and interpreting it in light of our context. Our starting point for preaching gospel in such moments is a justification by grace through faith that frees us for our neighbors. We have identified several features of the context that are salient for our gospel reflections. First, there are the individualized conceptions of faith in the wider culture of therapy. Second, there are the changing conceptions of religious life in a time of the disestablishment of the church and a rising pluralism in the public square that calls for a certain provisionality about our faith claims. Third, there is the problem of national will-to-power and the competing ideologies of the nation-state that sometimes complicate the articulation of gospel claims in public life. Finally, there is the reality that the church's own life bears witness both to the possibility of redemption and the reality of shared brokenness with the wider world. The goal here, however, is not merely to inventory the difficulties, but to begin to provide a framework for thinking theologically through the homiletical task that is preaching in the face of injustice. Therefore, to help preachers in their theological task, we offer five possible gospel commonplaces that can aid preachers in articulating the gospel in such moments along with some general implications for such preaching that these commonplaces entail.

Gospel Commonplaces for Preaching in the Face of Injustice

Commonplace One:
Gospel as God's word of liberating grace.

God's basic word to us in Christ is that we are set free. Justification by grace through faith means that we don't have to be prisoners of the "heart curved in on itself." God in Christ has set us free from that and, moreover, *for* our neighbor.[11] Yet this idea of justification is not merely a word for us as individuals. As a community of the justified, we ourselves are being redeemed from all of our shared attempts to justify our lives: whether through the gods of the marketplace and consumerism, the warrior god of the nation-state whose sacrifice of death first calls for the death of others, or the tribal gods of ethnic, racial, or gender exclusivism. Because we are justified by God's grace through faith, we are being made aware of our captivity to such forms of oppression. But more than that, we begin to see already how God's dawning promise of redemption and freedom is opened up. God's word, even in the midst of a world of oppression, is a word that is setting us free for new ways of being with each other.

Historian John Hope Franklin describes the time during the U.S. Civil War when news of the Emancipation Proclamation had begun to reach pockets of the South.[12] Long before the legal document or some facsimile had arrived two years before the war itself would end, word of the proclamation arrived and things started changing. Some slaves laid down their tools and began to walk together toward freedom—especially if Union troops were close by. Still others began approaching their so-called masters and began negotiating even then how they were going to receive wages for their work going forward. In one case the *Richmond Enquirer* related the story of a coachman who upon learning of his freedom "went straightly to his master's chamber, dressed himself in his best clothes, put on his best watch and chain, took his stick, and returning to the parlor where his master was . . . informed him that he might for the future drive his own coach."[13] The word of freedom didn't dispose of the struggle. No, the struggle was there and would continue through the days of Jim Crow and "separate but equal" court decisions. But already a word of promise was changing things and, even if just in fits and starts, moving toward a new day. God's gospel word works something like that. Its promise is even now beginning to free us for each other in a new way.

> **Implication**—Preaching in the face of injustice, like any other preaching, involves both justice and grace—in other words, prophetic preaching is still preaching the gospel.[14]

One of the great temptations of prophetic preaching is to turn it into moralism. Prophetic preachers should also ask themselves what the gospel is in this situation and how it addresses us in this situation of injustice. This does not mean obliterating the concept of justice or emptying grace, but holding them together in the gospel. Prophetic preaching should never sound like "it's all up to us" nor that thanks to grace "it just doesn't matter." Both fall short of preaching gospel in the face of injustice.

> **Implication**—Prophetic preaching trusts that the living word of God can do something to change situations.

This does not preclude or negate human action but is the gracious ground, promise, and magnetic hope of such human action. The gospel is not just an object of proclamation; its "subject" is God, who still speaks a living word to us. We may be tempted to split deeds from words, but the word of the gospel *does* something. Consistent with its own paradoxical disclosure in the cross of Christ, the gospel uses words to disclose how things really are and open up venues of hope and possibility that in turn empower us to engage and persist in struggling against injustice.

> ## Commonplace Two:
> *God neither wills nor needs injustice.*

Although we don't know everything about God (God still is a mystery), at bare minimum this gospel discloses to us that God wills our freedom and not our oppression. To claim that one's own or, worse yet, someone else's oppression is somehow necessary or willed by God is not only to make a claim that God makes or causes the bad, it is to contradict the most basic word that reveals who God is as the *justifier* of the ungodly.[15] The God of the gospel does not will anyone's oppression, least of all through the very warped sense of gender roles (spousal abuse), racial stereotypes (from chattel slavery through apartheid), or economic "laws" (from labor exploitation through classism)—all of which we human beings have tried perversely to enshrine as the result of an immutable divine will or order of things. How did Paul put it? "It is God who justifies, who is to condemn?" (Rom. 8:33b-34a).

To say that the gospel is God setting us free for each other is therefore to say that God neither needs nor wills oppression. Sometimes the lesson comes slowly. Years ago in Canada the government, working in concert with many Canadian churches, set up a system of residential schools designed to remove First Nations children from their family and cultural contexts and in turn enculturate them into the dominant Canadian Christian ethos. Although the churches claimed to be doing this for the benefit of the children and therefore out of some mandate to love, it became clear with every family separation, denial of cultural identity, and personal humiliation in these residential schools, there was nothing just about it. All the religious symbols and texts and actions in the world couldn't cover up the truth: the churches had become party to oppressing others. Of course, this difficult glaring truth was slow to dawn on the churches. They had a lot to lose in the courts for admitting their fault. Of course, it doesn't help that even now those First Nations people who won their battle for justice in the courts are still only too slowly receiving their compensation as they approach the end of life. But at least now Canadian churches have begun talking—talking to each other about how things could have gotten so bad, and, more importantly, talking to God in public forums of reconciliation and public acts of repentance about how they could have countenanced for so long what the God of freedom in Christ neither willed nor needed.

> **Implication**—Prophetic preaching embodying justice/grace sometimes needs to start with a theological analysis of a situation demanding response.

Preaching the gospel in the face of injustice is always profoundly contextual in that it uses tools of theological, economical, psychological, political, and/or sociological analysis to understand the context better in the presence of God in Christ. This contextual moment is important because it works against the idea that preaching exists to mystify present power relationships. Part of what such preaching does is to articulate that an injustice is not God's will but to call it what it really is.

> ## Commonplace Three:
> *The cross reveals both human injustice and divine compassion.*

What God does do is to enter the world of injustice to redeem it. In fact, the cross is the place where God is revealed to us, although *not as we would expect.* If we look to the cross, we see it first as a place not of divine power but weakness. In the cross, the power of oppression seems to win the day. The Roman Empire's symbol of social control, the cross of death, once again lifts up victims only as examples and warnings to indicate that the powers that be are not to be trifled with.

In Christian faith, however, the cross is revelatory in a much different way. On the one hand, the cross reveals humanity's complicity in suffering and death. No one escapes its powerful vortex: the empire itself, the religious leaders of the day, even the crowds are shown to be party to the oppression. At the cross, evil and oppression are shown for what they are: pervasive and profoundly interconnected. From top to bottom, such evil exacts a price both from those oppressing and those being oppressed. Oppression necessitates us turning on one another, dividing ourselves from each other, and cutting our losses by cutting ourselves off from our neighbors. After all, at the cross it was not God who needed a sacrifice, but human beings who demanded a scapegoat.[16]

But human capacity for collusion and complicity is not the only thing revealed at the cross. More importantly, the cross reveals something of God's own contrary way of engaging us. Rather than overwhelm the powers that be with the divine equivalent of shock and awe, rather than doing empire one step better with an overwhelming use of force, Jesus discloses a divine power of compassion and solidarity that our own enmeshment in oppression struggles to comprehend. God in Christ's commitment to us extends far beyond our own conception of power *over* to a strange power of compassion *with*. The cross demonstrates that God will not be waylaid, least of all by any human king-of-the-hill power scheme that assumes the necessity of One Winner and a mountain of losers. In the cross, God in Christ connects with all of us *at our weakest point* and refuses to walk away from any of us.

There's a fictional story about a family with an eccentric aunt from out of town. She was a kind of avant-garde artist, whose peculiarities had made her the object of jokes and derision among her kin. Sometimes she would invite her relatives to come for holidays or visits, always with exquisite promises of lavish hospitality, but none of the family ever accepted. Well, one year, instead of the normal invitation, the family was surprised to see two Christmas gifts had arrived from their crazy artist aunt. They opened the first package only to be disappointed. She had sent them a mirror rimmed with fluorescent lights. No matter how they hung it, the lit mirror only displayed all their blemishes, worry lines, and furrowed brows from years of disapproving looks. On the back, a cryptic message scribbled in their aunt's own handwriting: "As you really are." The family then proceeded to open the second gift. Inside was a carefully wrought, beautiful, hand-carved wooden frame. The family could tell from its flowing lines and stunning finish that their aunt had spent days working on this gift with her own artist's hands. When they tipped the frame forward, the family saw her signature and some more words: "I love you." For the longest time, the family was perplexed as to what to do. The mirror was worthless to them, the frame, priceless, but by itself useless—that is, until they found a note in the accompanying packaging. "These gifts belong together," the aunt wrote. And when the family placed the frame around the fluorescently lit mirror, the fit was perfect. And suddenly on the back, they noticed that the two messages on the joined gifts had become one: "I love you," it now read, "I love you as you really are."

The cross is a place of strange revelation for us. It reveals human brokenness and injustice for what they really are. At the same time, the cross speaks so much more. It reveals a God who enters that injustice and whose love is willing to redeem that reality for what it really is. In the process, we are confronted with a suffering love that jars us out of our top-down worldview: a worldview that demands only more separation, more suffering, more death. Yet this cruciform revelation *sub contrario* doesn't so much fix us, but it does, as theologian Douglas John Hall might say, "lighten our darkness."[17]

> **Implication**—Preaching gospel in the face of injustice emerges not solely from anger, but primarily from an articulation of human grief and loss experienced in the presence of God in Christ as disclosed in the cross.

Pastoral solidarity is its common ground, a solidarity that joins together parishioners by means of their shared pain, visible and invisible, connecting them to each other and the world God loves so much. A theology of the cross calls for preaching gospel in the face of injustice that moves beyond a finger-pointing anger to confess things "as they really are."

> **Implication**—Prophetic preaching is not about our moral capabilities, but takes account of the cross where we meet our brokenness and God's stunning solidarity. As such, the way forward cannot reject the humanity of anyone.

Implications for this in particular mean that we cannot demonize our opponents or use forms of argumentation that minimize the humanity of others. In this sense, prophetic preaching is also a kind of homiletical stewardship that understands God's use of our little human words in preaching "for the care and redemption of all that God has made."

Commonplace Four:
The resurrection of the Crucified One is promise.

It is only in the context of a *crucified* Lord that resurrection can be understood as a theological locus for preaching in the face of injustice. The biblical narratives go to great lengths to make the point. The Risen One is also the Crucified One. The stories make the point in the way stories do: Jesus makes a resurrection appearance, and Thomas is told to put his hand in Jesus' wounded side (John 21:27), or Jesus shows up to be with his disciples but knows first to show them his crucified hands and feet (Luke 24:34). The resurrection only makes sense as a proclamation of the gospel in the face of injustice when we recognize that it speaks of the Risen, *Crucified* One. If the cross is the sign of God's radical solidarity in the face of injustice, the resurrection is the sign that that cruciform solidarity continues even now.

Yet even this story speaks of more than can be said for now. After all, the resurrection is not a past-tense event, but the down payment on a promise. The resurrection of the Crucified One points to a future resurrection, a transformation in the shape of a promise. This is why Paul could speak of Christ as the "first fruits" of the dead. The resurrection betokens God's new age. It articulates a promise that God is not yet finished with this world. Rather than declare a past-tense event that can be dissected on some lab table of disinterested objectivity, it speaks of a mystery that opens up a future. But as a future, it is one that cannot ignore its cruciform history. The resurrection is thus a promise for life in the midst of oppression, violence, and suffering. The resurrection is cross-shaped good news about God's ultimate intentions.

How else do you explain the forward-looking hope of the civil rights struggles in the United States? Could it be that they understood how the resurrection was a cruciform promise? They had no outward reason for assuming that their efforts would meet with success. In fact, the only real visual evidence was that of opposition: marks and bruises from water cannons, bites from attack dogs, and much worse at the hands of local officials and nighttime vigilantes. But as they faced their opposition and were grasped by that promise, these walking-wounded strugglers for justice could sing hand in hand in the future tense: "We shall overcome some day. Deep in my heart, I do believe, that we shall overcome some day."

Implication—Prophetic preaching that preaches gospel in the face of injustice needs to be realistic about the hope it portrays.

It articulates a promise that takes account of the brokenness we still experience. Such promise does not obliterate struggle; rather, it enables endurance and resistance within it.

Commonplace Five:
The eschatological reservation means for now we know only in part.

Yet if we are to preach the gospel in the face of injustice, we also need to be modest about what we can claim to know. Paul says, "For now we see through a glass darkly, but then face to face" (1 Cor. 13:12a KJV). While there may have been a time as an established church when mainline Protestants could make pretensions to power, that time has passed. For Christians to articulate a cruciform gospel also means acknowledging that there are limits to what we can claim to know about God's will—if nothing else, because we also proclaim gospel in a public space that is not just Protestant, let alone even Christian. Proclaiming a gospel in the face of injustice will also mean being open to the claims of others in the public square. As the Lukan Jesus put it: "He that is not against you is for you" (Luke 9:50). Because the gospel is God's and not ours, we cannot claim to know it in all its fullness. The other side of the gospel as *promise* is that we are only now beginning to grasp it, or, better, to be grasped by it.

After the horror of 9/11, it was easy for many of us to hunker down. It was tempting to cocoon away in our religious enclaves. Even though religious persons of all kinds felt vulnerable for different reasons, it didn't have to turn out the way it did. One small mosque in Waterloo, Ontario, within days of the attacks, opened its doors and invited the community in. And in they came. Pausing at the door to remove their shoes, Christians, Muslims, and even thoroughly secular folks gathered in one place to learn more about each other. It seemed as if there was risk enough to go around—that's how tense it felt in those days after 9/11. Yet they gathered not because any one person had all the answers, but because for their different reasons they knew we had to talk and to begin hearing each other out. In the end, justice is a public matter for all creation. For those of us who proclaim a gospel of freedom, we know that it is that word that brings us to the table. Yet the public good to which the gospel impels us is also a *shared* good. Some of what that public good is emerges in the riskiness of admitting we need each other to discern it. We may not know everything; we may even disagree about the truth we have. But we are called to speak based on what we do know: the freeing love of God. So, in those moments like the gathering in the Waterloo mosque, we don't simply take off our shoes for custom's sake; we take them off because we are freed to speak visions of what justice can be for us right now; we take them off because when we do so, we are on holy ground. Within the eschatological reservation, we acknowledge that our gospel proclamation in the face of injustice is partial and provisional precisely because it is what it is: a word of promise, no more and no less.

> **Implication**—Preaching gospel in the face of injustice is open to a future that such proclamation cannot itself yet fully see.

Because of this fragmentary nature of what it knows, gospel proclamation is also open to others in dialogue about what God is up to. Such preaching should be profoundly realistic about evil and injustice and profoundly hopeful. Yet it should also be modest about how much it can name. Such preaching should leave us trusting the God whose promise animates our lives in the struggle, not claiming to see more than we can truly know about the details of God's mysterious will.

> **Implication**—Prophetic preaching is often times an in-church activity calling church people to live out their vocation of discipleship as citizens in a pluralistic world.

> **Implication**—Prophetic preaching is sometimes an out-church activity that either bears witness from an apologetic stance (i.e., explaining Christian faith in light of acts of discipleship) or articulates common grounds for working with people of other faith or nonfaith perspectives.

Implication—Prophetic preaching is not solely the prerogative of the clergy, but a manifestation of the ministry of proclamation that is given to the whole people of God.

The Spirit that is given with the prophetic word is given to all God's people, not just the clergy. This also means that the prophetic word should rightly aid God's people in becoming who they are already in Christ. As a practical matter, preachers should beware the Western myth of the lone ranger prophet.[18]

Clearly preaching the gospel in the face of injustice is no simple task. Yet in an age of disestablishment, it is now more important than ever that the task of prophetic preaching be taken up again with new discernment and insight in our changing context. Pastors can be sure that situations of injustice will rise from time to time and call forth from our all too human lips some kind of prophetic word. Yet we need not do so alone. God gives us the gospel to help us see our way forward even in times such as these.

CHAPTER 7

PREACHING GOSPEL
IN TIMES OF PUBLIC CRISES

Theologian Ed Farley has argued that ministers are tempted to reduce their theological work to the categories we might call "therapy" and "management."[1] At no time is this temptation greater for overwhelmed pastors than when they must preach in a time of crisis. Without any other resources to fall back on, we pastors in crisis situations can easily surrender to our culture's pragmatism to such an extent that we forget how good theology grounds our work in congregations. No doubt part of the temptation lies in the power of the cultures of management and therapy to explain and work. In a crisis, management can "get things done." And as for therapy, well, can we conceive of our tasks of crisis ministry apart from what we learned in Clinical Pastoral Care (CPE), and can our parishioners think of their own personal crisis realities apart from the cultural influences of Oprah and Dr. Phil? In other words, the very popular cultures of management and therapy have been found useful even among ordained ministers and Christian congregations and have proven indispensable in crisis situations.

This default position of management and therapy (and the seeming uselessness of theology) becomes especially critical in times of *public* crisis. Jet planes strike twin towers, a massive wave wipes out huge coastal regions in South Asia, or a hurricane guts a once-lively Gulf Coast community and pastors suddenly notice more people coming to church. Doubtless therapy and management will come in handy. Such crisis events stir up tremendous emotions, especially if we pastors find ourselves at the epicenters of such events. As pastoral caregivers we will need to call upon the best of the therapeutic arts. Similarly, when it comes to organizing and motivating Christian response to such crises, the language of management may in fact prove useful. The value of management and therapy in times of public crises cannot be gainsaid.

However, there is something more that preachers of the gospel are called to do. After all, there are social workers and counselors who can do more therapeutically than most of us can ever hope to offer. For that matter, local Red Cross and public officials have skills in crisis management that would put most of us to shame (with the possible exception of FEMA following Hurricane Katrina). Nonetheless, as valuable as these perspectives are, we need to remember that hands have been laid upon us preachers. And when that happened, no one said: "Go forth and offer therapy with remuneration on a sliding scale," or "Go forth and manage your organization like a CEO with an MBA and a pending quarterly statement." Instead, they likely said something akin to this: "Go forth and preach the gospel." For the purpose of articulating the gospel in such moments, we require good theology. To do the work of preaching in situations of public crises, we need to know what is and is not the gospel.

Discerning the Context

The question of knowing what the gospel is becomes exceedingly important in times of public crisis. In one sense the problem is concretized in the very terminology we are using to describe these moments of pastoral import.

Public crises are those that are bigger than the church. The people of God are aware of such events. Yet they compel attention beyond the boundaries of the parish proper. As such, they tend to demand our attention as the church-in-the-world, not just as church. Thus, in order to articulate what the gospel is, we need to be able to distinguish it from those "isms" and "ologies" that contend for what counts as truth in the public square.[2]

We do not need to look far to see that public crises are dealt with against a backdrop of many perspectives: ideologies, economic interests, political agendas, and cultural values. As an example, one might consider the aftermath of Hurricane Katrina. What started off as a "natural" disaster story quickly morphed into something different. Initially, the pictures of stranded New Orleans inner-city residents, primarily African American and poor, caused the United States to ask itself profound questions of race, justice, and fairness in American life. This was exacerbated by the media spotlight shone on the Bush administration's inability to marshal federal resources in a timely fashion for the sake of its own citizens. In response, however, the ideological machinery of the right shifted into its crisis mode. Clearly, they said, the misery that TV viewers were witnessing in New Orleans represented a failure of War on Poverty programs and classic liberal interventionism. Although the true inadequacies of the Bush government's disaster response would later be confirmed again in part of a different news cycle, the point had been made. The debacle of New Orleans was someone else's fault (the Great Society, cultural permissivism, local [read: Democrat] governments, the liberal media), not that of the most powerful government our planet has ever seen. Clearly, such a natural disaster was a crisis for all concerned; but because of the perspectives played out through it, the natural disaster also became a *public* crisis as a media event and a political/ideological/cultural issue of the first order. As such, when we as Christians react and respond to such public crises, we are not merely responding to the hurricane itself, but to the swirl of perspectives that both cloud and reveal the hurricane to us in government news conferences, radio talk shows, and network news coverage— all of which hope to use the event to advance their own ends. Unless we lived on the Gulf Coast or in New Orleans itself, we were always viewing the public crisis of Katrina through someone else's perspective. As a *public* crisis Hurricane Katrina had more than one eye.

Therefore, preachers need to separate out some of the issues at play. Savvy preachers of the gospel will need to anticipate contextual features that impact such public crises as perceived and relayed to the church-in-the-world. Two interrelated features of the context that merit gospel preachers' attention in times of public crisis are the corporate media and its culture of entertainment and the political agenda of the powers that be. This list of contextual features is not exhaustive, but it is suggestive enough to help us get started for thinking *theologically* (that is, not just in therapeutic or managerial terms) through the problem of preaching the gospel in times of public crises.

Public Crises and the Corporate Media's Culture of Entertainment

The outlines of this problem have been ably summarized by Neil Postman in his book *Amusing Ourselves to Death: Public Discourse in the Age of Show Business.*[3] Far from confirming the frequent accusation that the media suffers from a liberal bias, Postman demonstrates that the culture of entertainment has come to dominate the way in which news is gathered and presented in North America. This reality has a profound impact on the way we read crises in our therapeutic culture. Three elements of Postman's argument are useful for our purposes here.

First, the medium of television uses images to evoke feeling at the cost of understanding and to the detriment of discourse.[4] One need only think back to the media coverage of 9/11. The pictures were shown again and again. To be sure, there were voice-overs from experts who would provide important background about terrorism, the construction of skyscrapers, or the procedures of emergency personnel; but the towers kept falling over and over again in a kind of imagistic video loop regardless of what the expert commentators said. As is typical with most TV news coverage on a breaking story, there came eventually a series of 9/11 graphics to introduce each news segment along with a certain musical accompaniment, which, Postman points out, is usually used to cue TV viewers how to feel about a story. To be sure, there is enough about such cataclysmic events that leave us in wordless awe. Television, however, as the predominant medium by which we perceive the world and its "news," only rarely offers us the kind of depth understanding to match the pathos of images that cascade off the screen into our living rooms. Just as a good movie leaves us speechless when we are departing the theater, so also such pathos-laden, dramatized visual imagery without an equally strong mediation of understanding leaves us dumbfounded. Preachers of the gospel would be wise to attend to this reality as they reflect on their task. Our job is to relate the word to that entertainment-induced wordless awe.

Second, television tends to decontextualize the news by means of its disconnective logic *between* the stories that are covered.[5] For the most part the news is "one damn thing after another." Postman demonstrates this by pointing to the way electronic media tend to take information and disconnect it from its context. In the TV age, this is embodied by the "logic" that relates news stories seriatim on the news. Once the anchor has read a paragraph-long news story of chaos, crime, or calamity, he/she says with a smile: "Now . . . this." The result of this decontextualizing logic of TV news is a perspective on the world unable to draw meaningful connections to the past. Like the unblinking eye that is television itself, our consciousness as people formed by such media is that of the eternal present.[6] Again, such a loss of memory and context poses great problems for those charged with the task of making sense of situations in light of the gospel. While gospel preachers can't explain everything (God is a mystery, after all), we can place what we do know of this crisis in a wider context of the gospel whose "sense" may not be as entertaining as the "Now . . . this" newscast, but can provide a context of divine love and justice.

Third, the news is packaged in these ways not as to deepen understanding, but to sell eyeballs to advertisers by means of entertainment.[7] We, who live our lives in the presence of the cathode ray tube (or, now, the LCD or plasma screen) and tend to forget by living in an eternal present, are helped not to understand or to act, but only by virtue of the emotions elicited to consume. Just as in commercials, it is more important how you "feel" about the product, or the news, or even the anchors who read the news, than it is to understand, let alone act. Presenting news, including news of public crises, in a way that is entertaining will, they hope, keep you coming back to see it again. Perhaps this is why the human-interest story always comes at the end of the chaos, war, and wrangling of the half-hour news show. As long as you've felt something for thirty minutes; felt sufficiently "connected" to the anchor as a smiling, talking head; and felt mildly uplifted by the human-interest story at the end, perhaps you will be moved, not to do anything about the world, but to join the newsreader again tomorrow to see the news interspersed once again with three or four commercial breaks. Postman puts it this way:

> Entertainment is the supra-ideology of all discourse on television. No matter what is depicted or from what point of view, the overarching presumption is that it is there for our amusement and pleasure. That is why even on news shows which provide us daily with fragments of tragedy and barbarism, we are urged by the newscasters to "join them tomorrow." What for? One would think that several minutes of murder and mayhem would suffice as material for a month of sleepless nights. We accept the newscasters' invitation because we know that the "news" is not to be taken seriously, that it is all in fun, so to say. Everything about a news show tells us this—the good looks and amiability of the cast, their pleasant banter, the exciting music that opens and closes the show, the vivid film footage, the attractive commercials—all these and more suggest that what we have seen is no cause for weeping. A news show, to put it plainly, is a format for entertainment.[8]

Gospel preachers will need to tread carefully here. In a world where the news is another form of entertainment, where emotions are packaged in evocative images for the sake of keeping individual viewers "tuned," how do you preach truly *good* news? Part of our task will be to lead hearers through the media-induced emotional images more deeply into the difficult, weighty truth that is the gospel.

Public Crises and the Political Agenda of the Powers That Be

Public crises are also mediated in another sense. Crises are not merely reported for our entertainment, but are also used to further political agendas. Crises are used, in other words, by political and other powers to manage the public (of which churches are a part) and their perceptions.

Granted, there is a powerful element of political life that, like the televised media, is also geared toward entertainment. Political life in televised America is dominated by the cult of personality. Since the era of Ronald Reagan, political discourse has become more of a realm of personal disclosure and optics rather than policy debate.[9] As Roger Ailes, a former Reagan consultant (now, tellingly, the head of Fox News), put in a book title from the latter part of the superficial 1980s: *You Are the Message.*[10] The slippery slope of this self-disclosive communicational strategy, however, is revealed in the book's subtitle: *Getting What You Want by Being Who You Are.* So much for the gospel beginning with justification by grace through faith! The idea, which both Republicans and Democrats have adopted (please recall Clinton and Gore's speeches at the 1996 Democratic convention), is that "personality" *sells* a presidency just as well as it does a consumer product like laundry detergent.[11]

Beyond the impact of the entertainment culture on political life, however, it is important to note that even other elements of the media are used by governments and government officials in the service of advancing their political agendas. In their book *Manufacturing Consent*, Edward S. Herman and Noam Chomsky point to the selective way in which media news crises are used to further policy objectives:

> If the government or corporate community and the media feel that a story is useful, as well as dramatic, they focus on it intensively and use it to enlighten the public. This was true, for example, of the shooting down by the Soviets of the Korean airliner KAL 007 in early September 1983, which permitted an extended campaign of denigration of an official enemy and greatly advanced Reagan administration arms plans. As Bernard Gwertzman noted complacently

in the *New York Times* of August 31, 1984, U.S. officials "assert that worldwide criticism of the Soviet handling of the crisis has strengthened the United States in relations with Moscow." In sharp contrast, the shooting down by Israel of a Libyan civilian airliner in February 1973 led to no outcry in the West, no denunciations for "cold-blooded murder," and no boycott. This difference in treatment was explained by the *New York Times* precisely on the grounds of utility: "No useful purpose is served by an acrimonious debate of the assignment of blame for the downing of a Libyan airliner in the Sinai peninsula last week." There was a very "useful purpose" served by focusing on the Soviet act, and a massive propaganda campaign ensued.[12]

Here we see that political agendas also operate at the point of selecting and/or amplifying a story in the media. If government officials seize upon an event in order to characterize it in a way that furthers that agenda, they can and will. In some cases, such events are fabricated out of whole cloth (e.g., the Gulf of Tonkin) or exaggerated far beyond what a critical reading of the evidence warrants (e.g., "weapons of mass destruction" in Iraq). In the process, government officials in press releases and in sourcing stories for the media can set a powerful agenda for the media, the "public crises" it covers, and set a tone for the way the media covers them. This can also be applied to crises where there is a governmental prioritizing of appropriate victims:

> Conversely, propaganda campaigns will not be mobilized where victimization, even though massive, sustained, and dramatic, fails to meet the test of utility to elite interests. Thus, while the focus on Cambodia in the Pol Pot era (and thereafter) was exceedingly serviceable, as Cambodia had fallen to the Communists and useful lessons could be drawn by attention to their victims, the numerous victims of the U.S. bombing before the Communist takeover were scrupulously ignored by the U.S. elite press. After Pol Pot's ouster by the Vietnamese, the United States quietly shifted support to this "worse than Hitler" villain, with little notice in the press, which adjusted once again to the national political agenda. Attention to the Indonesian massacres of

1965–66, or the victims of the Indonesian invasion of East Timor from 1975 onward, would also be distinctly unhelpful as bases of media campaigns, because Indonesia is a U.S. ally and client that maintains an open door to Western investment, and because, in the case of East Timor, the United States bears major responsibility for the slaughter. The same is true of the victims of state terror in Chile and Guatemala, U.S. clients whose basic institutional structures, including the state terror system, were put in place and maintained by, or with crucial assistance from, U.S. power, and who remain U.S. client states. Propaganda campaigns on behalf of these victims would conflict with government-business-military interests.[13]

As a result, gospel preachers need to be aware of the ways in which the swirl of political interests are already having an impact on perceptions of crises as they are described in press conferences, sourced by government officials, and displayed in the increasingly oligarchic corporate media. Chomsky and Herman sum it up well: "Our hypothesis is that worthy victims will be featured prominently and dramatically, that they will be humanized, and that their victimization will receive the detail and context in story construction that will generate reader interest and sympathetic emotion. In contrast, unworthy victims will merit only slight detail, minimal humanization, and little context that will excite and enrage."[14] However, if we proclaim that all are justified by grace through faith, how can we as gospel preachers in a moment of crisis fall prey to such selective political agendas? If gospel and context belong together, preachers of that gospel must evidence a theological savvy about the public crises and their victims that governments prioritize and corporate media select for public view.

Discerning the Situation

Having identified two major contextual issues, we now turn to the outlines of situations of public crises themselves. We have argued earlier that situations that merit our attention homiletically tend to be either moments of "limit" or "decision." While it is possible to imagine public crises that provoke or call for a decision, most of the ones that we will face with some sense of temporal immediacy will be of the "limit" variety. These are, in other words, situations that expose our finitude and open up questions of divine mystery and transcendence. They prompt us to ask things like: How can God be God and situation X happens?

For the sake of doing a kind of pastoral triage of such situations, we could say that most public crises with which preachers deal fall along a continuum that looks like this:

Natural Disaster . . . . Human-made Crisis

The idea of the continuum is important for our take on such situations. On a continuum, natural disasters and human-made crises are not opposites, let alone altogether inseparable. In fact, as we saw with our description of the hurricane above, there can be a certain fluidity between the two. One could even take the analysis of such complex situations a step further: Is the emergence of a greater intensity in hurricanes recently a result of natural cycles, or does the human product of global warming play any role? This is where preachers will need to be vigilant. We will need to listen with great pastoral sensitivity to what people are saying and not saying in such crisis moments. Good contextual work requires knowing where people "are" in the face of such a crisis. At the same time, gospel preachers will also need to be current with what is happening in the wider world: mass media, yes, but also other new sources, scientific analyses, theological works, and so forth.

As part of this, pastors will need to use the best of good therapeutic and management/leadership literature.[15] In many of the best-regarded works, the authors avoid viewing matters of therapy and management apart from theology. To that end they are quite helpful. Nonetheless, we don't want therapeutic and management concerns so to dominate our homiletical work that we forget how preaching, good preaching, is first and foremost a theological task. In fact, we hope to show how thinking theologically in preaching offers a word both well grounded *and* pastoral precisely because it is good theology.

Therefore, the value of setting up a continuum for discerning situations, like the one above, is how it can help us figure out which gospel commonplaces, which theological *loci* might be most relevant for developing a situational sermon for a time of public crisis. A situation closer to the natural disaster end will probably require some theological reflection using a gospel commonplace about God's creation. A situation closer to the human-made crisis end of the continuum might need to include a gospel commonplace about sin, human corruption, and/or humanity's tragic state. Should one find oneself in a situation that encompasses both, then perhaps both *loci* will need to be a part of the gospel commonplaces used to address such a situation in light of the gospel.

Gospel Commonplaces for Preaching in Times of Public Crises

Once again, the commonplaces that we offer below are not exhaustive but suggestive. The particularities of a given crisis itself will probably require many theological *loci* that we cannot anticipate in this chapter. However, a homiletical theology of *your* crisis situation might profitably begin by thinking through the gospel commonplaces we've assembled below.

In a book of sermons collected immediately after 9/11, coeditor Martha Simmons described what she saw as four recurring strands of African American preaching that have surfaced again and again in times of terror and crisis: liberation; providence; the "sweet bye and bye," which brings us to grips with the "nasty here and now" (a homiletical eschatology, as it were); and the tension of being African American in contemporary culture (a kind of contextual theological anthropology?).[16] Although the four gospel commonplaces below are not identical to Simmons's four strands, they are inspired by them insofar as they touch on matters of providence and embody inherent tensions and paradoxes. The ideas are important ones here. In times of public crises, when by definition we do not know as much as we would like, we escape neither (1) the providential love of God nor (2) the tensions and paradoxes of our ordinary, broken, creaturely life. In these ways, Simmons's four strands are very instructive for the development of our gospel commonplaces. Preaching in times of public crises will need to begin with an acknowledgment of our limited knowledge about God in this situation and of our broken lives, which in light of such partial knowledge nonetheless seek a way forward; and come to terms with what it means to entrust ourselves to God's providential love. Yet in the process, we will as always need to do so in a way consistent with the good news of the gospel, a gospel that holds together both death and resurrection.

> ### Commonplace One:
> *God is a mystery in the sense that the God we meet in crisis is both hidden and revealed.*

One of the most important things we can say in a moment of crisis is that we don't know everything, least of all where God is in it. A crisis happens, and our minds are reeling. Does God give us this crisis as a moment for meting out divine justice? Does God come to rescue us from the crisis? Does God share in our grief, without really causing or fixing the crisis at all? We grope in our language for the truth. Yet in truth, there is so much we don't really know. Paul seems to have anticipated the necessary humility of a homiletical theologian when he wrote in quite a different context for his congregation in Corinth: "For now we see through a glass, darkly; but then face to face" (1 Cor. 13:12a KJV). This side of heaven, Paul seems to say, what we can know and say about this mysterious God we invoke has limitations—all the more in times of public crises. We need therefore to be honest in the pulpit in such times: God was and still is a mystery.

Of course, we should remember God's mysterious nature as soon as any crisis hits. On a human level to be in a crisis is to be in a kind of fog. There is a reason why so many people react to a crisis with a kind of numbed, dumbfounded shock. As we write these words, there is an unfolding news story about thirteen miners in West Virginia. Throughout the event as relayed by the media, we have discovered that what we know and don't know about the situation matters considerably. News reports began with word that the miners were trapped in a mine that had been cited for several state and federal safety violations. While people watched and waited for news about the thirteen miners' fate, they prayed for a miracle. At first, the local townspeople were thrilled when word came that twelve miners had been discovered alive. People celebrated their miracle. Yet the celebration proved premature. Because of a miscommunication, it became known three hours later that all but one of the missing miners were found dead. The miners' families were devastated. Their joy had turned to anger. Some said their miracle had been "taken away." Still others pointed to the history of safety violations at the mine and said: "This was no act of God, but an act of man." The different kinds of language they used point to the realities we face as preachers in crises. We don't know everything on a human level, let alone the whole counsel and mind of God. So, above all, a little homiletical modesty is in order in most public crisis sermons. God may be personal, but God is not just any other person. God the Infinite One, and especially God in the midst of a crisis, is still a mystery to us finite human beings. God's ways are not our ways; and for now we can see only in part.

Jesus seems to have understood this. In Luke's Gospel, Jesus receives word that Pilate had mingled the blood of some Galileans with their sacrifices (Luke 13:1-5). Anticipating his hearers' readiness to turn such a crisis into a pronouncement of divine judgment, Jesus points out that those Galileans, just like those upon whom the tower of Siloam had fallen in Jerusalem, were no worse offenders and therefore no worthier than anyone else of divine punishment. Please notice he doesn't blithely solve the mystery (this is why those Galileans or these Jerusalemites "got it"); Jesus refuses to bring the divine mystery down to our all-too-human moral calculus.

Martin Luther made it a point to distinguish between what he called the hidden God and the revealed God. With Luther, the distinction is never a dualism, always a paradox. There are some things about God we cannot know or understand. The hidden God is and remains mysterious to us, beyond our knowing and beyond our human grasping. And yet the other part of the paradox is also true. There is the revealed God, the God disclosed to us in Jesus Christ. To the degree God is disclosed to us in Christ, we can know something, if not all things, about God. And what do we know? Something of the divine love disclosed to us in the cross and in the resurrection of the Crucified One. So, in the end, the God we meet in times of crisis is both hidden and revealed.

> **Implication**—Preaching the gospel in times of crisis requires above all homiletical honesty.

Just as in a funeral, where a preacher is wise not to claim to know the deceased better than he or she actually did, so also in crisis we need to take care not to overstep what we can know about the mystery that is God. Sometimes in our desire to be helpful, we say more than we ought. In preaching gospel in times of public crisis, our sermons should be rightly bounded by divine mystery and not pretend preening certainty.

> ### Commonplace Two:
> *To the degree God is revealed to us in Christ, it is through the cross, a revelation of God precisely where we would not expect it, in suffering.*

In fact, if we wish to ask the question of where God is in crisis, we need to begin by looking at the cross itself. One reason we too quickly get into theological problems is that we assume the revelatory moment will be an obvious one. Where was God? We might venture a few answers:

- *Answer #1*: Sure some died, but God protected others. (Problem: If so, then why didn't God find time to "protect" the ones who did die?)
- *Answer #2*: Sure some died, but God was testing the faith of the survivors. (Problem: What kind of God kills or allows others to die just to test the faith of another? Would such a god be moral? Loving?)

- *Answer #3*: Sure people died, but God was working through the rescuers. (Problem: If God works that way, couldn't God have gotten on the job sooner, using "people" who rescue to prevent rather than just to respond?)

An underlying problem with all these theological perspectives on a public crisis that involves suffering is that we assume that God is not in the suffering but somehow over it. God somehow causes, allows, or even circumvents suffering. Therefore, if God is revealed, it is through some *power* either to bring about suffering (typically as punishment/discipline/means of growth), allow suffering (God could have stopped it but chose not to), or get around suffering (God's power consists in the ability to get around suffering by empowering/enabling human agents). However, a theology of the cross asks a different question. What if God is not "over" suffering but paradoxically "in" suffering? In that case, the question of the revelation of God, who is a mystery, would be centered not so much in the language of power over (whether in meting out suffering, allowing suffering, or circumventing suffering) but in the symbol of the cross itself. What such a theology says is that suffering, paradoxically, is the place of divine revelation, instead of power "over" being the place of revelation.

Douglas John Hall, a theologian in the United Church of Canada, has attempted to develop this seminal insight into a comprehensive, contextual theology. In his book *The Cross in Our Context: Jesus and the Suffering World*, Hall seeks to make such a theology of the cross into the centerpiece of his work. His view is that we talk about the cross not just to bandy about atonement theories as rationalizations for the necessity of Jesus' death, but that the revelation of God in Christ *on the cross* is the "key signature" for all theology. As such, if the issue is one of revelation (How is God revealed to us in this crisis moment involving suffering?), the issue is not so much about figuring out what display or aspect of power is the key to divine revelation in that moment (disciplining, allowing, or circumventing with rescue), but assuming that the cross itself is God in Christ's "key" mode of revelation. A theology that does so, says Hall, can avoid all the problematic power plays that have messed up Christian theology hitherto: for instance, triumphalism, proselytism, and the like. Why is this an issue? Because a church that cannot discern God's revelation in the cross surely will not be able to discern God's presence in a suffering world like ours. To be blind to suffering as a locus of divine revelation is tantamount to missing God in Christ altogether.

The source of Hall's view is what he calls the "thin tradition" of theology of the cross. While it has had a few advocates in church history, its primary exemplar is Luther. In the Heidelberg Disputations, Luther set out such a theology in a series of propositions. Without a theology grounded in God's revelation *in the cross*, we can tend to a theology of glory, just another example of Christian triumphalism or will-to-power. And when we minister with people who themselves are overwhelmed by suffering, who themselves struggle to see God at all, such a theology may be the only real lifeline we can throw. How is this so? Luther argues that a theology of the cross calls a thing "what it really is." A theologian of glory argues that suffering only appears bad but is really something else: for example, "You are undergoing suffering right now, but God is actually only disciplining you and showing you God's love by doing so." A theologian of the cross, by contrast, calls suffering what it really is but nonetheless sees it as the place where God, not in glorious power, but in cruciform weakness, is revealed.

Naturally, such a view requires some careful thinking. First, when a theology of the cross talks about suffering, it does not valorize it. Suffering is bad, not good. And a theologian of the cross must call something what it really is. Moreover, suffering is not something that is *prescribed*, but *described*. Life in this world is already marked by suffering. However, that does not mean that human beings *should* suffer, least of all in order to get masochistically closer to God. The mystery of God, however, is that God is revealed *sub contrario*, under God's opposite, which means that if we human beings are to see God, it is not in displays of power that are merely magnifications of human powers (e.g., the evil causing this crisis is big, but God is bigger still), but in its opposite: God comes to us *incarnationally* in cruciform weakness.

There are times when the idea is abundantly clear to us. In Advent and Christmas we love to revel in God's incarnation in the baby Jesus. We all love to preach about the strange paradox of divine love revealed there. He is not born of wealthy parents, nor in a palace, nor even in a time when God's people have it all together. Instead, he is born in a marginalized family, in a manger, and precisely at a moment when God's people is under the lash of the Roman Empire. The mystery of the incarnation, however, is not one that confines itself to homely manger scenes. Instead, as some have put it, the incarnation runs all the way from the stable to the cross.[17] Luke plays this out with Simeon's two-part prophecy in Luke 2:29-35. This young Jesus presented in the temple will be "a light of revelation," yet he will also be a sign of "contradiction" and "a sword will pierce through your own soul also." In other words, even baby Jesus has a cruciform shadow over him in Luke's Gospel.[18] Matthew has his own way of bringing the point home in the second chapter of his Gospel. Three Magi come to share presents. The first two bring gifts fit for a king: gold and frankincense. Yet the third gift is also part of the story: myrrh . . . for this baby's *burial*. At this epiphanic moment of revelation, even the Magi's gifts point to a coming death. From the beginning of incarnation to its end, God in Christ is revealed in cruciform weakness and suffering.

How important is this for times when we preach in crisis? If we are to preach the gospel in moments of crisis, our task is not to touch lightly on suffering and transform it like magicians into something else. Rather, our preaching task may just be to head more deeply into it. For where else will we expect to see our Lord revealed in such crisis moments, if not in the cross of suffering? Thus, to preach the Gospel in crisis is to acknowledge that a theology of the cross is key throughout.

Implication—The temptation pastorally in such moments will be to sacrifice "meaning" in a crisis to certain visions and presuppositions about divine power. Preachers in a time of crisis need to be wary of claiming authority for views that end up with a divine-human relationship that tends toward the arbitrary and the masochistic.

> ### Commonplace Three:
> *Suffering in a crisis can neither be justified by divine omnipotence (whether God "causes" it or "allows" it) nor omniscience (God knows what's best for us) let alone explained by reference to a suffering God, only resisted through the aid of God's sustaining and empowering compassion in the midst of that suffering.*

We have argued that two important gospel commonplaces for preaching in times of public crises are that God is a mystery (revelation) and that suffering is precisely the place where that mystery begins to be disclosed. To make such homiletical moves, however, requires acknowledging the theological problems that suffering causes—especially in crises. If one of our first questions in a time of public crisis is "Why?" surely the next to follow must be something like this: "If God is good, then how can such things happen?"

To ask such questions is to broach the theological problem of "theodicy," or the justification of a powerful and loving God. As we saw earlier in the news stories about the West Virginia coal miners, the thought is never far from our minds.

Of course, if someone dies, we *can* keep the issue in an altogether human frame of reference. Who is responsible for the death of the twelve coal miners? We might again venture a few answers:

- *Answer #1*: Was it the miners themselves? They accepted a higher hourly wage than most of their neighbors, but did so knowing that risks were higher for them. They weren't the first folks in mining country to die from a disaster in a coal shaft.

- *Answer #2*: Was their employer responsible for their deaths? The mining company had been cited many times, and quite recently, for safety defects in the mining operation. Surely a corporation that failed to act on those warnings has some liability.

- *Answer #3*: Or was the government responsible? The federal and state mining safety agencies had cited the mine but did not shut it down. The government had means at its disposal, but in the age of governments getting cozy with corporations, there was a failure to engage in proper enforcement of the mining rules.

Clearly, there are many ways in which we could look at a crisis like the West Virginia mine disaster and ask whether these deaths could ever be "justified" given human responsibility and liability.

However, it is also true that such moments of crisis draw God into their vortex, too. If we say that God is all-powerful, for example, does God bear any responsibility for events that happen on the divine watch? If we claim that God actively directs or plans everything, we have to say that God caused the event. Yet even if God merely *allows* such events to happen, God is also not off the hook. If God had sufficient power to act and yet chose not to, even for the best of reasons, God still bears something of a passive responsibility. Perhaps then we argue that God's power is manifest only through the best efforts of human agents ("God has no hands but our hands . . ."), for instance, the rescuers, but even then God does not escape total moral culpability. Couldn't God have worked a bit harder through those charged with their rescue? If so, why did God fail to do so? In these cases we are asking questions about how to justify *God's* action or inaction. We are in the process assuming that to "be" God entails having the potential to act with sufficient power to alter the situation.

In our day, it has become increasingly difficult for us to speak of God in such terms. At times we become practical atheists. It is tempting to get God "off the hook" altogether by positing some kind of world where God exists only at a distance. Yet we who call ourselves Christians should have a problem with such views. We confess that God has not stayed far away. In fact, in Christ, God has come close enough to share profoundly in the world's pain. If we, moreover, confess the cross as God's great revelatory moment, we cannot afford the luxury of keeping God's hands clean by keeping God at a safe distance from the world's pain. Christ crucified won't let us get God off the hook.

Perhaps, then, the issue is not one of the relationship of God and pain (God in Christ seems to have been reconciled to that already!), but of God and our conceptions of divine power. If models for understanding theodicy bump up repeatedly against ways of holding on to God's goodness *and* God's power, perhaps we need to reconceive what God's power actually is.

Theologian Wendy Farley offers a way of thinking through theodicy for situations of radical suffering. In her book *Tragic Vision and Divine Compassion*, she suggests that we surround the issue of radical suffering too much with matters of sin and moral culpability.[19] What we end up with is either human beings who are blamed for their own radical suffering and/or a God who on the basis of some divinely wrought cosmic law metes out punishment. She views that as a theodicy shaped by an exclusively forensic or penal metaphor. As a counter to that forensic/penal tradition of theodicy, she offers a "tragic vision" complemented by an emphasis on divine compassion as the mode of divine power.

Tragedy and Radical Suffering

In invoking tragedy as her basic metaphor, Farley seeks to draw a line larger than the legal/forensic framework the tradition has used to deal with the theodicy problem. The "tragic" for Farley includes the especially thorny theological problem of undeserved suffering. To be sure, tragedy accounts for elements of human freedom and accountability, yet without lapsing into a deterministic view that puts human beings in the role of puppets. In tragedy the tragic hero is free to make choices but moves, tragically, from good fortune to bad fortune. In the end, the tragic hero goes down in flames, but not without a kind of Promethean defiance. The tragic hero makes his/her choices in good faith *despite* the tragic outcome. There is no real "happy ending" redemption here (perhaps a better model for thinking about undeserved suffering anyway), but there is a sense in which the integrity of the tragic hero in that defiance bears witness to its own limited, provisional truth in the face of suffering and even death.

Divine Compassion and Theodicy

The compassion side of Farley's work refers especially to the divine side of the theodicy problem. To speak about God's compassion, of course, would seem to touch on the impassibility of God (God, as an eternal being, is not subject to suffering and feeling as human beings are). Nonetheless, it is fair to use this metaphor to describe the "effects" of the divine life on humanity. God's compassion is such that creation is its manifestation. In compassionate love God creates alterity, something *different* from God. It is moreover out of this compassionate love that such otherness in the limits of finitude and fragility begets its tragic possibility. God's compassion, for example, creates lions and gazelles, but because this compassion begets alterity, God does not control/dominate creation and its myriad relationships. The fact that lions eat gazelles becomes part of that alterity that God in God's compassionate love respects for what it is. If this creation arises out of God's compassion, it is decidedly not a manifestation of sovereign "power over." Moreover, as a continuation of God's compassionate love, redemption consists not in solving problems from the top down, but in a kind of "suffering with" (*com*-passion, or in German, *Mit-leid*) that enables two things for those who experience radical suffering: (1) the "power" to resist the causes of suffering (whether personally or politically); and (2) the "power" (Farley uses the word *course*) to resist the power of suffering to dominate others.

Farley offers this helpful summary toward the end of the book:

> Compassion does not overcome the power of destruction, any more than Jesus came down from the cross. The power of destruction is real; the lives, hope, sanity, and goodness that are maimed by cruelty can never be replaced or atoned for. But it is the power of divine compassion to endure, to be deathless, to be resurrected even from the ashes of despair and death. There is a resilience to divine compassion that the superior strength of evil cannot finally overcome, however real its victories.[20]

To be sure, Farley's work leaves some questions. "Tragic vision" may not always be adequate to the problem and hers is not even the only understanding of the tragic.[21] Still, it is important to ask how this kind of language might affect our preaching in times of public crises. Farley does help us think about language for dealing with undeserved suffering. There is something quite homiletically appealing about the quality of divine compassion in creation and redemption that redefines power as something different from domination. Descriptively, this comes much closer to the kind of power God offers in creating a world where suffering tragically exists and redeeming a world, albeit without top-down interventions. It also offers a helpful complement to our second gospel commonplace above. When God does meet us in suffering, God does bring power. It may not be the power to blow suffering away, but may just be a different kind of power: a compassion that strengthens for resistance.

Implication—Preaching gospel in times of crisis requires navigating a way between at least two rocky shoals: a naked, unreflective view of divine power and an anthropocentrism that reduces everything to "us" and what we can do. Gospel preaching in such situations requires careful homiletical work that can't be reduced to breezy pieties and Hallmark cards.

> **Commonplace Four:**
> *The God who comes to us in the suffering of the cross does not provide a fix for suffering, but provides "enough" through word and sacrament to resist in the face of tragic crises.*

Now that we have thought through three key theological *loci* for preaching in times of public crises, we return to one gospel commonplace of great importance: divine providence. Please notice, however, what we have done so far. We have argued that the disclosure of God in crisis is not obvious, but a mystery of hiddenness *and* revelation. What is revealed, moreover, is revealed first and foremost through the cross, which is the revelation of God in Christ we can hold on to in the midst of suffering in a crisis. Christ crucified as God's self-disclosure of love for us, however, causes us to revise our notions of theodicy. We need not "justify" God in terms of reconciling God's omnipotence understood as "power over" and God's love. Instead, we can now view God's power as a power "with" in the created context of tragic existence and borne by a power of God's compassion, which enables resistance to suffering. With this, we can now finally talk about providence in a more meaningful way.

It is tempting in times of crises to talk about God's providence in either superstitious or overblown ways. The former tends to invoke the miraculous to talk about providence. After 9/11 not a few stories circulated around the Internet about people who miraculously did not go to work at the World Trade Center that day or did not take one of the doomed flights. Yet talking about divine providence in such ways only reopens the theological problems we identified earlier. If this is how God "provides," why did not God do so for nearly three thousand people who did die that day without miraculous warnings or flight cancellations? If as pastors we are not inclined to resort to the miraculous to resolve church-funding shortfalls, personal health crises, or parking lot problems, it seems a little incongruous to do so in a time of crisis. In times of clearer thought, we know that the "miraculous" superficially conceived is not God's main mode of providing for us. Yet another tactic is to hold to a view of providence that asks us to disbelieve the reality we do know: "It may *seem* that the terrorists and their evil ideology have determined events, but God is the one actually in control." This view of providence asks us to bracket the evidence of evil/suffering that we see in the name of a less visible consideration: a divine providence understood as pure sovereignty and omnipotence. While such statements may make us feel good, they do not escape the problem identified earlier. If God does "provide" out of such sovereign power, is not God actually culpable? Does this view not actually draw God's love into question in the name of holding on to God's omnipotence in divine providence? Clearly, we need to allow the three previous commonplaces to help us reformulate what God *does* provide in moments of crises.

In a general sense, we can talk about God's providence in connection with creation. God does provide by creating and sustaining the world in which we live. This view is, of course, also consistent with the view of God's power articulated earlier. God's relation to the created order is one of compassionate love. It is not the power of "control over," although it is a sustaining, compassionate power supportive of life and its flourishing. More specifically, however, it is important to remember the way in which God provides by coming close to us in Jesus Christ. In the compassionate weakness of the cross, God provides presence and strength in the very face of absence, meaninglessness, and death. For us in the church, the primary means of such provident grace are word and sacrament. Through the word, Christ comes to be with his people in the face of all suffering and adversity. In the word-sign of the sacraments, that self-same word comes to be with us in water, bread, and wine. Outwardly, these gracious signs of God's providence may not appear to be much. They are certainly not miraculous, nor do they testify to some invisible power over that seems to be contradicted by the crisis events that leave us reeling. Yet in simple human words, in elements like water, bread, and wine, Christ does come in weakness once again. And when Christ does come to be present in this way, God does provide *enough*.

This playful truth about divine providence is embodied wonderfully in a Jewish song about the exodus, *Dayyenu*, roughly translated, "That would have been enough for us." The song is sung as part of the Passover seder. As a remembrance of the difficulty and the provision of God in the exodus, it is a wonderful example of the kind of providence we are envisioning. The middle part of the song goes like this:

> Had he sustained us in wasteland,
> And not fed us with the manna. *Dayyenu.*
> Had he fed us with the manna,
> And not given us the Sabbath. *Dayyenu.*
> Had he brought us to Mount Sinai,
> And not given us the Torah. *Dayyenu.*[22]

Carmine DiSante, a student of the Jewish influences on Christian liturgy, sums up the meaning of these stanzas with great insight. He writes concerning these lyrics:

> These words might seem a rhetorical exaggeration were it not for the testimony of millions upon millions of Jews down the centuries who never ceased to sing the *Dayyenu*, even in the ghettoes and concentration camps. In their mouths it expressed not the nihilistic illusion that turns everything to absurdity, but the flash of meaning glimpsed beyond all the meaninglessness and giving the courage for continued belief and struggle.[23]

Perhaps we Christians can begin reconsidering what providence means from such a view. God does not so much provide by being "bigger" or "stronger"; rather, God provides by giving enough to get us through the struggle. We who receive by divine provision God's grace in word, water, bread, and wine, know that these "signs" may seem weak or small. Yet in our frail human words become God's word, in the font of water, and in the one cup and one loaf we do receive, God does give *enough* to sustain us in the struggle. And such a providence is valuable chiefly because it continues to corroborate God's own self-disclosure through

Christ on the cross. Oh, it may seem like weakness and foolishness, yet for those of us being provided for, it is nothing less than God's strange wisdom and power. Though these may not seem like much, they are . . . *enough.*

> **Implication**—To talk about God's providence in a moment of crisis is to speak with a certain degree of fragility and provisionality. As with the first commonplace, honesty about God's provision is important. Even our songs of divine providence are sung in the "key signature" of the cross.[24]

Optional *Loci*: Gospel Commonplaces for Crises across the Continuum

We have argued above that crises that call forth preaching may well fall across a continuum from natural disasters to human-made ones. Clearly, in cases where such issues predominate, preachers will want to develop gospel commonplaces for their crisis sermons that speak to them, too. For example, a crisis sermon resulting from a tornado or tsunami will likely need to reflect theologically on the natural order and what it means. In talking about the natural order *theologically*, it will be important to distinguish Christian understandings of creation from those that surface in other parts of our culture where nature is often alternately romanticized and exploited, let alone the insurance industry, which in the hope of getting off the hook of financial liability calls certain uninsurable events "acts of God"! When a crisis is the result of human action, clearly some sort of commonplace about human sin will be in order. The gain, of course, in focusing on times of crisis with the commonplaces above, is that it wrestles with the problems of suffering in a crisis *apart* from purely human conceptions of suffering as penalty/guilt. Yet there may be times when one does have to address crisis moments where human beings are indeed culpable. The act of discernment in this case will be in determining whether a given crisis moment is truly the result of such human culpability. A Christian televangelist may like to muse out loud that a hurricane strikes New Orleans because God has taken offense at the immorality of its inhabitants. Yet such bizarre notions of the penal view of suffering are quickly lampooned by comedians who, seemingly with greater insight, point out that the notorious French Quarter, unlike most of the city, had been spared. Jumping too quickly to the option of human culpability in such moments may make it hard for us to be heard in those times when a gospel commonplace about human sin and injustice may just be called for. Good preachers will recognize that both nature and sinful humanity live in profound tensions and not simply use every public crisis as an occasion to horsewhip the general public.

Conclusion

So where does that leave us? Because you've read this chapter, you are further along than last time a crisis came knocking at the door of the church. You have already begun to reflect generally on crisis situations and what they might mean theologically. God forbid that you should ever have to preach another sermon on Sunday after a Tuesday when three thousand died in twin towers or when tens of thousands die after a killer tsunami crashes ashore across a whole region of our globe. Nonetheless, we who preach have been around long enough to know that suffering in crises does come. Perhaps next time, when people come surging into our churches wrestling with these same questions, we'll be ready to engage them with a gospel that speaks with an equal profundity of depth and hope.

CHAPTER X

PREACHING GOSPEL GOING FORWARD

The reality of preaching gospel in situations is that you cannot foresee every situation. As preachers of the gospel, we will find ourselves repeatedly surprised with situations that emerge and thus challenged to do the kind of contextual-theological reflection we need in a given moment. The Scriptures say, "How beautiful are the feet of those who bring good news" (Rom. 10:15, paraphrasing Isa. 52:7). We maybe should get used to the idea: preaching the gospel in such situational moments will require *"thinking* on our feet" as we bring the good news so we can move forward together as God's people in the world. How beautiful that would be!

This is why we have numbered this chapter X instead of chapter 8. The point here, however, is that this chapter is still being written; like the X in algebra, it is a mystery still being solved. You, the reader, are in all likelihood a pastor or someone preparing to preach situationally. In such moments, it is now *your* job to be a residential theologian where you are. Consider chapter X to be your invitation to become a homiletical contextual theologian in your own right. It is now up to *you* to bring gospel and situation together.

Chances are, you have probably grasped something of our approach in the previous chapters. Here, however, we make our method a bit more explicit so you can go and do likewise.

Imagining Situations beyond the Stained Glass

As we have discovered, situations can be of many different types. There are many kinds of situations where you might be called to speak gospel. Perhaps you will get a call from the local school principal to speak at a high school baccalaureate (yes, this still does happen in some communities!). Maybe a local veterans group will ask you to say a word at a Memorial Day observance. It could be that your jurisdictional body (synod, diocese, presbytery, conference, etc.) is seeking a way forward by debating an issue such as same-sex blessings and has provided time for you to say a word on the issue. Then again, perhaps you've been invited to speak at an ecumenical or interfaith thanksgiving service. These moments are all situations where you need to be able to "think on your feet" for the sake of the gospel, to be a residential *public* theologian beyond the stained-glass confines of the local church. They are by definition difficult moments. On the one hand, they are certainly not "in-church" preaching. On the other hand, the invitation extended to you to speak is done so with at least some sense of your office and role in a community of faith. What does gospel sound like in moments like these? What gospel commonplaces might be helpful in the public square? In our work with students in class, we usually suggest the following steps:

1. Start with Your Understanding of the Gospel.

We have proposed that one can use the doctrine of justification by grace through faith as a beginning for gospel reflection. This does not mean that the gospel is *reduced* to this one doctrine— far from it. In fact, throughout this book you will have noticed that our gospel commonplaces, while including justification, did not stay there, but pushed gospel reflection into theological *loci* such as the doctrines of providence, eschatology, theology of the cross, and so forth—all depending on the nature of the situation under discussion. This is to reiterate what we first stated in chapter 1. The doctrine of justification gets the gospel "rolling" for us; it shakes loose situations and helps us to reflect on the gospel through them. For some people, the starting point of the gospel may be located someplace else. Some may even wish to claim that there is a timeless core of the gospel that only needs to be applied to situations. Whatever your understanding of the gospel is, you need to clarify it for yourself. Whether you preach using a situation as a starting point for an "occasional" sermon or you are even beginning with a lectionary text in the normal fare of Sunday-to-Sunday preaching, a clear understanding of the gospel will help you.[1]

In our class at Waterloo Lutheran Seminary, we actually assign a short, two-page paper on a "theology of the gospel" at the beginning of the term for our senior students. Because we teach at an ecumenical Lutheran seminary, not everyone's theology of the gospel sounds as broadly Reformation Protestant as the one we've laid out in these pages. Students and pastors interested in exploring these matters should read some of the homileticians we've cited in this chapter and might consider the bibliography in the back of the book. What you will discover is that there are a wide variety of theologies of the gospel and myriad ways of relating those gospel understandings to the contexts and situations we have described in this book. In the end, *you* are the residential theologian where you are. Our goal in this book is to stimulate you as a preacher of the gospel not to do the same thing as we do, but to go and do *likewise*, that is, relate your understanding of the gospel to the contexts and situations of pastoral ministry that call forth gospel speech.

2. Move Toward the Context and Situation.

In this second step, we think in explicitly pastoral terms. A pastor knows that situations have both personal and social impacts. A pastor also knows that sometimes decisions need to be made about whether to respond at all.

Let's begin with the second issue. When being asked to speak, preachers need to discern on the basis of the gospel whether it is appropriate to respond positively to an invitation to speak at all. Just because the local arms manufacturer wants to have a clergyperson pray at the rollout of their latest high-tech missile does not mean that you have to say yes. There will be times when pastors, in the name of the gospel as they understand it, will need to say no. We in the church have had a history of cozying up to power and dressing up violence, money, or some other aspect of the status quo in the seeming sanctity of clerical gowns and stoles. Because our preaching is grounded in the justifying gospel of the crucified and resurrected Lord who himself preached the good news of *God's* kingdom, we must realize that there are times when we say no and times when we say yes.[2]

Yet there is another side to this issue. While being asked to speak at a baccalaureate is a bit of a holdover from the days when Protestant pastors were essentially chaplains to the wider culture, nowadays we are well on our way to being *disestablished*.[3] In such moments, we find ourselves increasingly having to speak not only in ecumenical, but also in *interreligious,* contexts—places like baccalaureates, where the desire to discern some sense of meaning in such moments comes face-to-face precisely with multiple religious traditions and diverse groups of persons. If we say no to every such moment, do we miss an opportunity to speak in the breach? Pastors will need to weigh such moments. Postliberal types are correct in pointing out that our churches have had a history, at least as far back as Constantine, of confusing the gospel with the great oughts and duties of an often violent and well-moneyed cultural will-to-power.[4] Yet, as those charged to preach gospel for the sake of the world God loves so much, we must acknowledge that there are still places where God says yes to the world. While the culture cannot simply set the terms for the gospel, it would be equally foolish to say that the yawning chasm of meaninglessness and the yearning for some wider, transcendent horizon has nothing to do with what God is up to in Christ. Despite what some would say, God does not send Christ into the world to "absorb" the created world into some separately righteous and meaningful God-world. God in Christ, rather, yields up godlikeness, takes flesh, and enters our world in all its godforsakenness to redeem it. As those living on this boundary between gospel and culture, we have the unusual task to discern where to say yes and where to say no when such invitations to speak arise.

Assuming we have determined it might be a good idea to speak at a baccalaureate, how might we consider the relevant pastoral issues involved? We have argued broadly that pastoral concern touches on both personal and social dimensions. Both need to be understood for us to think about which gospel commonplaces to use.

On the one hand, the invitation to speak at a baccalaureate will prompt questions of pastoral concern. The faces of the high school graduates from one's own congregation may leap to mind. What do these persons need at this rite of passage? What do their families need as one of their own transitions from childhood to adulthood? These are pastoral issues that touch on the quality of care we give. They quite naturally have an impact on the way we see the baccalaureate situation.

On the other hand, pastors are also aware that such moments also have a social shape and impact. The baccalaureate straddles the public secular and religious dimensions. Most such moments will take place with a view toward a secular, public institution: the high school.[5] There was a time when religious leaders in the community had a de facto relationship to the schools: baccalaureate services, yes, but also prayers at school board meetings, football games, perhaps even a cameo at the junior high "sex" talk. In many communities, however, there is more than just a little unease about such events. In Canada, clergy at public events like these are sometimes asked to design prayers that address God in only the most general, nonconfessional terms possible, if at all. This is to say that, in many places, the baccalaureate is a kind of "vestige" of the age of cultural Protestantism. This, naturally, makes such invitations to speak quite a bit more complex and touchy—especially if we wish to avoid being mere representatives of civil religion. What do we say when the pastoral role seems clear, but the public one less so? How do we articulate something of the gospel in a public space where Christian speech is vestigially privileged but otherwise disestablished in a religiously pluralistic and largely secular context? Thus, we may also need to thematize not the "unity" or our identities, but also the differences that precisely shape this moment.

3. Determine Which Gospel Commonplaces (Theological Loci) are Germane to This Particular Situation.

Having thought about our sense of the gospel and the pastoral shape of the particular situation, we begin to think about relevant theological *loci*, our gospel commonplaces. At the point of saying yes to the invitation, we have already decided that the justifying word of the gospel frees the world to be the world. In light of that prior theological move, other *loci*, other "gospel commonplaces," become more prominent.[6] Because the baccalaureate is an event outside of the church and includes a broader swath of the world God so loves, it would seem to touch on matters of *creation*. We come to such moments not solely on the basis of a particular ecclesial identity, but because of our share in God's creation. Because we come to such moments as human beings, it might also likely touch on matters of *theological anthropology*. At shared transitional moments like a baccalaureate, we are aware of our shared humanity and also something of our finitude, perhaps even our brokenness (are not such moments ones of both joy and regret?). Assuming that such situations, where we become aware of our own finitude/brokenness, can also open up questions of transcendence and divine purposes, we may also find ourselves drawing on commonplaces like *eschatology* and *providence* as well. Eschatology may be important because we sense as we move through transitions that all this is heading somewhere. There is some sort of end, not just in the sense of a "conclusion," although that is there, but also a "purpose," as in the question, "To what end?" Providence may also be useful, because we wonder what it is that God is up to in such moments. Our list of theological *loci* here is not exhaustive, merely suggestive. Somehow these gospel commonplaces might help us articulate something of a public meaning for such moments.

Please notice that one theological *locus* not mentioned in the list above is anything related to Christology and/or soteriology. How can this be? A preacher of the gospel certainly cannot deny the centrality of Christ for Christian thinking and theology. At the same time, Christ himself points to God's broader purposes not only in creation, but in God's final purposes at the end of all things in eschatology. Because we are operating in a secular world that, while broken, still is God's good creation, we don't need to turn every such occasion into a come-to-Jesus moment. Indeed, if the apostle Paul is right, Christ's intention in dying and rising is not to take the kingdom for himself (a kind of Christomonism), but to hand it all over to God (1 Cor. 15:24-28) so that *God* can be all in all. There is nothing intrinsically wrong with mentioning Jesus (after all, apart from his death and resurrection, Christian preachers would have nothing to say), but it is also not intrinsically *necessary* either in the sense that Christ orients himself to the world in the kenotic path of yielding self-effacement to the eschatological end that *God's* good purposes become manifest. To turn Christ into a kind of legalistic *necessity* for Christian preaching is to miss precisely the self-effacing grace he embodies both in his kenotic incarnation and self-yielding final destiny. It is Christ's own nature to point away from himself to God. Perhaps to preach the gospel of Christ is not just to preach about him as a topic, but also to preach *in him*—in other words, speaking in Christ within his self-effacement toward the divine purpose, so that God may be "all in all."

4. Determine the Gospel Aim of This Sermon.

As a practical matter, preachers need to decide how their sermon will use one or more of the above gospel commonplaces to do their work. One might choose one commonplace above and preach thematically. One might also, however, link together two or more of the above *loci* to develop a way of reflecting publicly about what God is up to in such moments as a baccalaureate.[7] One such baccalaureate sermon might envision an aim such as this:

> This corporate moment of transition to adulthood reminds us of God's broader purposes in giving us life, where we discover ourselves as both broken and yet beloved. Yet as we raise our heads toward the emerging horizon of our lives, we also find ourselves strangely gifted by God along the way and begin to discern a future that includes all sorts of others: across racial, ethnic, or religious differences.

What we have here is a basic structure for reflecting about the moment that takes in not only matters of divine transcendence, but *grace* in relation not just to ourselves, but others—indeed, God's ultimate purposes in continuing to create and provide for us going forward.

5. Prepare For and Follow Up on This Gospel Occasion.

This fifth step is actually quite important for the work of situational preaching, although we have barely touched up on it until now. The situational sermon is not a discrete, separate occasion. Ideally, pastors will prepare congregations for such moments. Whether it's the normal conversations in pastoral care where a preacher learns what's on people's hearts and how they see certain situations, or whether preachers actually convene corporate discussions on matters of corporate import, it is always wise to view situational preaching within the wider horizon of pastoral ministry. How often does the gospel word of one sermon "fix" a problem? One suspects such moments are rare. What is more likely is that our practices before and after a sermon open up the possibility of a wider ownership of a situation. Pastors know this intuitively around funeral ministry. Time spent with a family prior to a funeral is not merely some fishing expedition for what to say in the funeral sermon. Just the opposite! It is the pastoral care in those moments that helps frame hearing the gospel in the shadow of death, grief, and loss. Similarly, sometimes what we say in a funeral sermon cannot possibly be fully absorbed in the moment. When the word comes, says John, it comes to "dwell with us," or as the Greek implies, "to pitch its tent" among us. The follow-up after the funeral is an ongoing relationship where the word continues to do its incarnational, grace-bearing work. Thus, situational preachers would be wise to consider how to prepare for and how to follow up after every situational sermon.

So how about you? What precedes a baccalaureate sermon? What comes after? Situational preachers understand that the gospel is more than a momentary flash of light. Part of our task is to discern how God's gospel word shapes everything from pastoral care to youth ministry to committee work. As a fifth step, situational preachers will want to plan ahead for and follow up after moments when the relationship of gospel and situation are brought into focus.

Conclusion

So here you are at the end of chapter X prepared now for your own baccalaureate. With this chapter you yourself are "graduating" in a sense. If you have always been interested in thinking gospel through situations of parish ministry, we hope we have helped to make your work more interesting. Consider it another in a long series of theological degrees for you, the theologian in residence. If, on the other hand, you have hesitated at the threshold of preaching situationally, we hope now you have felt graced enough to move across it. We noted earlier in a kind of paraphrase of Henri Nouwen that "Ministry happens in the interruptions." Well, that's what situations are. They interrupt our cycles of texts, our lectionaries, our seasons, our programming goals, and demand our attention. But a situation does not have to be a scary departure from standard operating procedure. Indeed, by focusing on the relationship of gospel and situation, you may just find your normal, everyday, run-of-the-mill scheduled preaching enriched by a clearer sense of the good news as well. In either case, you are and will be a theologian of the word. Someone either has or may well still lay hands on you and say, "Go, preach the gospel." And you will—sure, sometimes falteringly, even with knees knocking. But just remember: whenever the angels bring a difficult charge, they also bring a gift to be shared. "Fear not," they typically say, "Fear not, for I bring you tidings of great joy." And no matter how unwieldy or unplanned or even fearful the situation, those joyful tidings of the gospel are always worth talking about.

APPENDIX FOR PREACHERS

HOW TO USE GOSPEL COMMONPLACES FOR YOUR *KAIROS* PREACHING MOMENTS

Throughout the book, we use the word *commonplaces* to describe theological *loci* that are useful for articulating the gospel in light of situations that call for *kairos* preaching, a timely word from the pulpit. But what do you *do* with gospel commonplaces in an actual situational sermon?

Because situational preaching cannot always foreground a biblical text, such a sermon focuses instead on how the gospel needs to be unpacked theologically to deal with that situation within its context.[1] The gospel commonplaces we list in each chapter are, therefore, a bit like theological talking points for different types of situational sermons. Depending on how you view the *kairos* preaching task, you could use our gospel commonplaces, or *loci*, in at least two ways.

Choose a Gospel Commonplace for a Main Idea

One way would be to choose one well-suited gospel commonplace and use it as a theme, topic, or single "point."[2] Such preaching has a long and venerated history. Assuming that you tend to think of preaching in terms of a theme, you could find one of our gospel commonplaces to be a help to putting your sermon together. Since we want to understand theology through story, image, and metaphor, we already take you partway down that path in the preceding chapters. Each commonplace represents not only a theological *locus* or idea, but tries to show concretely what that gospel commonplace looks like as it makes an impact on our shared life. We envision each commonplace as if it were a *theological* sermon help.

Homiletician Ron Allen suggests that in such preaching moments one of the things we need to decide early is whether a single idea or topic is one we might preach deductively or inductively.[3] A deductive sermon is shaped like a triangle pointing upward. Its theme or topic is stated early (see figure A.1, below). The goal of such a sermon is *applying* that main idea to life and experience.

It is deductive because it deduces its applications from a truth already agreed upon. A deductive sermon "leads from" (*de*-duction) a gospel commonplace to explore and apply its implications in a situation. It moves from the general to the particular. An inductive sermon, by contrast, starts with particular experience in all its diversity. Because it is shaped like a triangle pointing downward, it does not signal its "main idea" until the end (see figure A.2). In other words, it moves through the complexity of life and experience to *arrive* at its main theological point as a kind of insight that dawns on the hearer(s).[4]

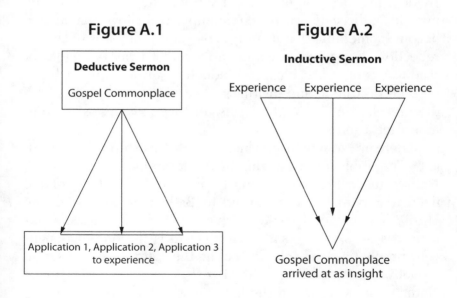

Figure A.1

Deductive Sermon

Gospel Commonplace

Application 1, Application 2, Application 3
to experience

Figure A.2

Inductive Sermon

Experience   Experience   Experience

Gospel Commonplace
arrived at as insight

An inductive sermon leads to or into its gospel commonplace (*in*-duction) by reasoning from the experiential particular to the general.

Both of these "single idea" approaches to a gospel commonplace have merit. A deductive sermon based on a single theological theme or topic would be most helpful in situations where a situational preacher needs to remind hearers of a shared gospel commonplace that hearers already hold.[5] In reminding hearers of such foundational aspects of the gospel, the homiletical task is really to make a deeper theological connection with something already acknowledged as central in a faith community. Sometimes, however, single-idea preachers may need to explore elements of a context that help us see faith not in an expected way, but in a new one. In those moments, an inductive model can be situationally helpful. An inductive sermon, because it begins with the complexity of experience and situations, can have the advantage of maximizing the participation of hearers. By delaying until the end of the sermon the disclosure of the main idea, the single gospel commonplace, it allows that idea to become something that hearers arrive at on the basis of shared reflection. For a gospel commonplace that hearers might not readily accept at first blush, an inductive-sermon approach can be both disarming and inviting to hearers as participants with the preacher in coming to an insight that a given gospel commonplace affords.

There are situations in which an inductive approach is most apt. The Bible offers an instructive example. In 2 Samuel, Nathan the court prophet must convince King David of the need to repent for what he did to Bathsheba and Uriah the Hittite. Of course, if you're Nathan, your rhetorical task is far from easy—especially since King David is the one who signs your prophetic paycheck. So Nathan the court prophet uses an inductive approach to get the king to "convict" himself. Once Nathan tells King David the fictitious story of a rich man who stole a poor man's one beloved sheep for his own party, David flies into a royal rage of judgment and announces that this rich man should die. At that point, the prophet can add the timely words at the end: "*You* are the man." By the end of the exchange, the king is participating in the way the truth has dawned "inductively" upon him.

Whether one proceeds deductively or inductively, the focus of this kind of situational sermon is usually on a single idea: a topic or a theme represented by a gospel commonplace. A preacher who holds that a sermon should be about one such topic or theme will find productive opportunities among the gospel commonplaces we identified above. Yet single-idea sermons, whether deductive or inductive, are not the only option for the person wishing to preach the gospel in a situation.

Choose Two or More Gospel Commonplaces to Structure Theological Reflection

Another way to use our gospel commonplaces would be to chain two or more of them together within a sermon's development. In this case, one would need to think of a logical movement that holds them together as a development of thought. In our experience, situational preaching usually requires "thinking through" a situation, which means a progression of thought that the gospel walks us through in light of a moment. It is interesting that the Bible often does this, too, in its own narratives and reflections. In Acts, for example, the apostle Peter has the tough task of explaining the events of Pentecost to Jews gathered in Jerusalem from all the parts of the known world (Acts 2:22-33). It's interesting to notice that Peter doesn't offer a single-idea sermon.[6] Instead, he engages the questioning crowd in that Spirit situation with a *progression* of thought through a series of theological statements not unlike our commonplaces:

- Jesus came from God and did marvelous things among you, as you know (v. 22).
- But you rejected him, and he was crucified (v. 23).
- Of course, that didn't stop God: the Crucified One was raised according to God's promise (vv. 24-32).
- That means God's new resurrection age has begun in which the Spirit helps us understand crucified/resurrected life in what we see and hear today (v. 33).

In Peter's speech we have a series of at least four gospel commonplaces used to make sense of the situation in Jerusalem on that Pentecost (Does Jesus' exaltation to God's right hand in v. 33a deserve a separate theological *locus*?). They are set in a logical progression appropriate to the moment. But it uses more than one commonplace in order to make sense of the situation. Underlying Peter's speech is a kind of "theo-logic" that helps him do his rhetorical work through each *locus* or commonplace in the progression.[7]

Preachers should perhaps look at our gospel commonplaces in a similar way. They represent theological elements that can be linked together to make sense of a situation in light of the gospel. Since many sermons superimpose organizing schemes and stock plots (thesis/antithesis/synthesis, narrative, not this/or this/but that, etc.) on the sermon, preachers who use our gospel commonplaces should take care to note *how* the commonplaces might link organically. Fred Craddock, in his book *As One without Authority*, argues that such shifts in thought are usually marked by words like: "however, but, and."[8] David Buttrick argues that a series of "moves" should follow a kind of conversational logic.[9] Using two or more of our gospel commonplaces will require thinking through the connections between them in order to use them well. After all, what we are doing is articulating the gospel as we think our way through a situation together.

The Gospel Goes Ahead of You

Back in our chapter on the gospel, we explored the tension of Mark's emerging understanding of it in 1:1-15: the gospel was about Jesus Christ, Son of God (1:1), and yet when Jesus himself comes preaching, it's the "gospel of *God*," the good news of the kingdom (1:14-15), that enables repentance/belief in the gospel. Even in our earliest New Testament Gospel, the gospel is more than simply a timeless formula (Christ and him crucified, or death and resurrection, or some other summation of the kerygma), but a way of seeing ourselves forward with respect to what God is up to in Christ through the power of the Holy

Spirit. It is perhaps then fitting that in this appendix we return to Mark, this time to his conclusion to grasp what is at stake going forward. After all, Mark's theologically curious beginning in 1:1-15 can only be topped by his puzzling ending in 16:1-8. Mark, this Gospel that helped us begin our reflections on the gospel, concludes with a resurrection commission that not even the otherwise faithful women are able to carry out: "They said nothing to anyone, for they were afraid." What do you do with a Gospel that begins with such a rich sense of the gospel (1:1-15) and ends in fearful silence?

In one sense, the tradition has tried to fix this problem. Fairly early on an alternative ending to Mark appeared in the tradition (the so-called "longer ending of Mark" in 16:9-20). However, most scholars agree that this material is not really Markan and was indeed added later. In another sense, the emergence of three other Gospels testifies to the attempt to "fix" Mark's ending. Some have argued that dissatisfaction with the Markan conclusion in 16:1-8 was a driver for the writing of other Gospels, especially the Synoptics, which otherwise hew closely to Mark's version. Our own preference, though, is to view this theological problem against the horizon of Mark's own Gospel. Why would *Mark* wish to end his Gospel of the gospel this way?

New Testament scholar Mary Ann Tolbert has offered an interesting idea. Rather than providing the typical narrative closure that one would expect, Mark purposefully ends with a failed telling. Readers of the Gospel, having witnessed Jesus' own preaching and sowing of the gospel of God, his way of suffering and the cross, as well as the (seemingly) thwarted news of his resurrection, are now put in the role of the ones who are enabled to complete the commission. From the beginning, readers knew what this Gospel of the gospel was about. It is now Mark's reader through whom the sown gospel comes to fruition. The young man at the tomb told the women that the Risen One would go ahead of them to Galilee (16:7), the very place where Jesus first began preaching the gospel of God (1:14). At the end of the Gospel, the gospel likewise goes ahead of us—God's message continuing to do its thing, even through us, for the sake of the wider world.

No doubt, the gospel still goes ahead of us. It is not a thing we can control or master. It is, however, something that draws us forward beyond fear to faith, beyond even our Markan text to whatever Galilean ministry lies ahead of our fearful, limited vision. Although the gospel is often reduced to controllable formulae, it is the nature of the gospel itself to draw us forward into new times and places where it can be renamed. This is in fact the open-ended theological task of gospel proclamation. It goes beyond settled formulae, just as the Scriptures themselves do, to help us articulate that gospel for a new time and new place. The gospel is not the text, nor is it simply an eternal kerygmatic formula; it is, as theologian Edward Farley says, a new world. He puts it this way:

> Gospel is not a thing to be defined. It is not a doctrine, a delimited objective content. The summaries in Acts and in Paul of what is proclaimed, the formulas of the kerygma, attest to this. Phrases like "the kingdom of God," "Jesus as Lord," "Christ crucified" do have content, but that content is not simply a quantity of information. To proclaim means to bring to bear a certain past event on the present in such a way as to open the future. Since the present is always specific and situational, the way that the past, the event of Christ, is brought to bear so as to elicit hope will never be captured in some timeless phrase, some ideality of language. Preaching the good tidings is a new task whenever and wherever it takes place.[10]

Naturally, this brings us preachers out of our comfort zones. Yet it could be that this is precisely the point. The gospel may have a core, but it also has a contingency, a context, a situation, that draws us beyond the "settled" to something new.

Two Final Rules for the Road for Gospel Preachers Going Forward

Yet if this is true, it does require a little further homiletical reflection. To that end, we would like to offer two last bits of advice to gospel preachers going forward into ever-new situations. One has to do with the sermon finding its unity in the gospel itself and the freedom toward which it aims. The other is concerned with *limitations* of what that gospel does in any situation this side of heaven.

1. The Freedom Toward Which the Gospel Points Provides Its Unity

Any sermon that chooses a single theme will go a long way to being unified and focused. A sermon that links together commonplaces as a way of thinking through a situation will need to find a way to stay unified (and not devolve into separate sermonettes). In both cases, however, what really unifies a sermon is not just a single idea or even a singularity of purpose, but the gospel itself. Although we preach with gospel commonplaces to think through a situation, we don't just do so for the sake of good thought. The gospel is not simply information; it does something. It is, in fact, the good news of God's doing in Christ through the power of the Holy Spirit. Whether in a theme or in a linked series of commonplaces, a gospel sermon oriented toward a situation should do more than provide information, even correct theological information. Perhaps it should, in its own provisional, limited way, *free* its hearers for the situation. As Farley says, it is about "opening a future."[11] Sometimes it does so by breaking open a closed perspective on the world.[12] Sometimes the gospel does so by boldly bringing a hidden or secret reality into the light. On other occasions, the gospel merely reminds us of our deepest-held values in such a way that it allows us together to peer over the edge of the abyss and really *live* nonetheless. Whatever the gospel sounds like in a given situation, it is deeply about such freedom—a freedom that while grounded in the good news about Jesus also, like Jesus, points beyond itself to the purposes of God's reign for all creation in the life of the Spirit (e.g., as we saw in Mark 1:1-15 and in Acts 2:22-33). The gospel is no mere formulaic recitation, nor just a rehearsal of the Scripture's narrative, and certainly not a one-size-fits-all-situations idea. The gospel cannot be heard in any mere repetition of the words we have always used. The good news of the radical grace of God will take different forms in different contexts, and part of our task as preachers is to discern the form that will help people hear good news for them. The gospel *moves*—and more than that, it moves *us* toward freedom in the face of the situations in which we find ourselves.

2. For Now, the Gospel Points Toward Freedom as the Horizon

And yet, for all the joy freedom brings, it is important to view the gospel we preach under one limitation. This side of heaven the freedom the gospel brings to situations is not the perfect fix of TV commercial solutions: the shirt collars are not spotless, the "before" people who become "after" people do not look like supermodels, and the family drowning in bills before the magical refinancing often don't even get to keep the house. This side of heaven, the freedom the gospel moves us toward is a horizon; it is provisional. It is not perfection, but in the shadow of death at a funeral, in the threshold of a decision in sickness and in health, when the congregational cashflow does not suffice, or in whatever situation—it is *enough*. Perhaps it is a bit like communion. What we get is this: a morsel of bread, a sip of wine, and yet the Risen, Crucified One along with it. And whether we receive all this in solemn remembrance or with sacramental presence, one thing is true: just like the gospel, it isn't everything this side of heaven, but here and now in this situation, it is *enough*.

Conclusion

So here we are, called to preach the gospel in this time and place. Thanks be to God, not every sermon will require us to think on our feet in the same way. Still, there are times, moments of interruption, where real ministry requires us to be theologians of the gospel. You can be sure that we won't get it all right. We see, as Paul says, through a glass darkly. And yet the gospel itself goes ahead of us: a word of Christ, yes, but a word that, like Christ, empties itself out into the world God loves so much, pointing in its own justifying, liberating way, toward the new thing God is up to, right here, right now.

NOTES

Introduction

1. Henri J. M. Nouwen, *Reaching Out: The Three Movements of the Spiritual Life* (Garden City, N.Y.: Doubleday, 1975), 36. Nouwen actually references some words he heard from an unnamed older saint: "You know . . . my whole life I have been complaining that my work was constantly interrupted, until I discovered that my interruptions were my work."

2. Ronald J. Allen talks about this in great detail in his book *Preaching Is Believing: The Sermon as Theological Reflection* (Louisville: Westminster John Knox, 2002).

3. The claim we are making here has to do with the form and content of language in sermons as actually preached. We are not necessarily arguing for a separate Christian grammar and culture along the lines of George Lindbeck's work, *The Nature of Doctrine: Religion and Theology in a Postliberal Age* (Louisville: Westminster John Knox, 1984). While we believe the gospel does challenge culture profoundly, especially cultural elements that deny or obscure God's grace, we are also convinced that the culture and human language are actually useful for gospel proclamation. With a nod to Origen, we will gladly "plunder the Egyptians" if it enables the articulation of the gospel in a given context and for a given situation.

4. For a survey of nineteenth- and twentieth-century thought on this issue, see Stephen Sykes's excellent work, *The Identity of Christianity: Theologians and the Essence of Christianity from Schleiermacher to Barth* (Cambridge: Cambridge University Press, 1973). This is in part why Sykes abandons the language of the "essence of Christianity" for the term *identity*.

5. Sallie McFague's *Metaphorical Theology: Models of God in Religious Language* (Philadelphia: Fortress Press, 1982) is certainly a good starting point for literature that relates theology to understandings of language.

6. This is not a new idea for homiletics. Some have argued that preachers should use theological terms in a focused and illustrative way in order to reclaim theological language for church discourse. Paul Scott Wilson pursues this idea in his book *Imagination of the Heart: New Understandings in Preaching* (Nashville: Abingdon, 1988), 41–42. Others, however, recognize the limitations of some of the more abstract language of theology and encourage preaching to be theological by using story, image, and metaphor in connection with "theological definitions" that are themselves concrete and suitable for oral discourse, as one finds in David Buttrick's important work *Homiletic: Moves and Structures* (Philadelphia: Fortress Press, 1987), 29–30.

7. There are some important exceptions. Some homiletical books do look at how to use theology *in* preaching. William J. Carl III in *Preaching Christian Doctrine* (Philadelphia: Fortress Press, 1984), and Robert Hughes and Bob Kysar in *Preaching Doctrine*, Fortress Resources for Preaching (Minneapolis: Fortress Press, 1997), wrote to help preachers develop sermons on theological topics. LeRoy Aden and Bob Hughes (*Preaching God's Compassion,* Fortress Resources for Preaching

[Minneapolis: Fortress Press, 2002]) and Lee Ramsey (*Care-Full Preaching* [St. Louis: Chalice, 2001]) have sought to address the gap between preaching and *pastoral* theology in particular.

8. In rhetorical theory commonplaces can refer to common themes used across different kinds of speeches or, as with Aristotle, patterns of argumentation or inference. Rhetorician Stephen D. O'Leary offers a helpful summary of the issue as it pertains to contemporary topical theory and millennial preaching in his book *Arguing the Apocalypse: A Theory of Millennial Rhetoric* (New York: Oxford, 1994), 21–25.

9. There are three translations of and introductions to different editions of Melanchthon's *Loci*. Clyde Manschreck translated the 1559 edition in *Melanchthon on Christian Doctrine: Loci communes, 1555* (New York: Oxford, 1965); Wilhelm Pauck translated the original 1521 edition in *Melanchthon and Bucer*, Library of Christian Classics, vol. 19 (Philadelphia: Westminster, 1969); and J. A. O. Preus translated the 1543 edition in *Loci Communes 1543* (St. Louis: Concordia, 1992).

10. The language here of "limit" and "decision" goes back to the work of David Buttrick in *Homiletic*, 408–11.

11. This difficulty is demonstrated ably in Sykes's historical study of what used to be known as the "essence of Christianity" in Schleiermacher, Newman, Harnack, Loisy, Troeltsch, and Barth in *The Identity of Christianity*. Is it possible to discern an essential sense of what the gospel is apart from features of context, community, and historical moment? In part because the language of essence has become so problematic in the twentieth century, Sykes speaks of "identity" even in his title. For a theologian who takes up this sticky problem of articulating the gospel from a contemporary stance, see the work of Edward Farley, *Practicing Gospel: Unconventional Thoughts on the Church's Ministry* (Louisville: Westminster John Knox, 2003).

12. The document of the U.S. Catholic Conference of Bishops, *Fulfilled in Your Hearing: The Homily in the Sunday Assembly* (Washington, D.C.: USCC, 1982), 1, makes this quite clear by quoting on its first page from Vatican II's Decree on the Ministry and the Life of Priests #4, "The primary duty of priests is the proclamation of the gospel of God to all." More recently, the issue of the content of that gospel, especially as it relates to justification, has emerged in theological discussions between Lutherans and Roman Catholics, "Joint Declaration on the Doctrine of Justification," http://www.lutheranworld.org/Special_Events/OfficialDocuments/jd97.EN.html, accessed February 23, 2009.

13. New Testament scholar Stephen Westerholm traces a fascinating history of the apostle Paul's influence and understanding through Augustine, Luther, Calvin, and Wesley in his book *Perspectives Old and New on Paul: The Lutheran Paul and His Critics* (Grand Rapids: Eerdmans, 2004), 3–87. Although these Protestant theologians stand at the head of diverging theological traditions, they take with great seriousness a largely Pauline understanding of justification by grace through faith. Naturally, such views of Paul have come under serious question of late, especially the degree to which one can relate to a kind of Lutheran reading of "law" through Paul: e.g., Krister Stendahl (*Paul among Jews and Gentiles* [Philadelphia: Fortress Press, 1976]) and E. P. Sanders (*Paul, the Law, and the Jewish People* Philadelphia: Fortress Press, 1983]), among others. Westerholm includes their critiques in his work, however, and makes an interesting case for elements of continuity that run from Paul through to the above-mentioned Protestant theologians.

1. Theology of the Gospel

1. Neil Postman, "The Parable of the Ring around the Collar," in *Conscientious Objections: Stirring Up Trouble about Language, Technology, and Education* (New York: Vintage, 1992), 66–71.

2. For example, Carl Braaten states that the gospel is more than any one, single doctrine: "A theology of the gospel can be developed only within a cluster of supporting concepts." See Carl Braaten, *Justification: The Article by Which the Church Stands or Falls* (Minneapolis: Fortress Press, 1990), 95.

3. John Reumann, *"Righteousness" in the New Testament* (Philadelphia: Fortress Press, 1982), 185.

4. *Webster's New World Dictionary of the American Language*, ed. David B. Guralink, 2d College ed. (New York: William Collins + World, 1978), 659.

5. See Robert A. Kelly, "Successful or Justified? The North American Doctrine of Salvation by Works," *Concordia Theological Quarterly* 65, no. 3 (July 2001): 224–45.

6. George Forell argues that Luther's doctrine of justification should be understood in terms of "axiological eschatology." This is to say that justification represents an eschatological reality that is already experienced as proleptically present without altering the ambiguities of life in the present: "It is because God is coming towards us, because the 'Dear Last Day' is approaching, that we can live here and now as sinners and righteous at the same time." See Forell's "Justification and Eschatology in Luther's Thought," *Church History* 38, no. 2 (June 1969): 169.

7. For a brief discussion of the eschatological dimension in Luther's understanding of faith, see Walther von Loewenich, *Luther's Theology of the Cross*, trans. Herbert J. A. Bouman (Minneapolis: Augsburg, 1976), 89–91. Heiko Oberman also highlights the eschatological, even apocalyptic, side of Luther in his *Luther: Man between God and the Devil*, trans. Eileen Walliser-Schwarzbart (New Haven: Yale University Press, 1989).

8. Krister Stendahl has critiqued classic Lutheran-Augustinian readings of Paul in this light in "The Apostle Paul and the Introspective Conscience of the West," in *Paul among Jews and Gentiles* (Philadelphia: Fortress Press, 1976), 78–96. Others have argued Stendahl's critique focuses on an overly pietistic/existentialist interpretation of Augustine and Luther. Homiletician David Buttrick has sought to reconsider doctrines like justification in more social terms, namely as a ground for freedom and resistance, in his book *Preaching Jesus Christ,* Fortress Resources for Preaching (Philadelphia: Fortress Press, 1988), 31–32.

9. We recognize that significant Lutheran theologians would disagree with the way we are putting this in the name of the distinction of two kingdoms. Our intent is not to undo this important distinction, but to follow through on some of its insights in a contemporary context. To examine the details of this argument, see Robert A. Kelly, "Are We Serious? The Liberatory Possibilities of the Doctrine of Justification," *Consensus* 19, no. 2 (Fall 1993): 41–70, and "Lutheranism as Counterculture? The Doctrine of Justification and Consumer Capitalism," *Currents in Theology and Mission* 24, no. 6 (December 1997): 496–505; reprinted in Wolfgang Grieve, ed., *Justification in the World's Context: Documentation No. 45* (Geneva: Lutheran World Federation, 2000), 209–12.

10. The Augsburg Confession (German), Article IV, in *The Book of Concord: The Confessions of the Evangelical Lutheran Church*, ed. Robert Kolb and Timothy Wengert (Minneapolis: Fortress Press, 2000), 38, 40.

11. Eric W. Gritsch and Robert W. Jenson, *Lutheranism: The Theological Movement and Its Confessional Writings* (Philadelphia: Fortress Press, 1976), 42.

12. von Loewenich, *Luther's Theology of the Cross*; see also Gerhard Forde, *On Being a Theologian of the Cross: Reflections on Luther's Heidelberg Disputation, 1518* (Grand Rapids: Eerdmans, 1997); Douglas John Hall, *Lighten Our Darkness: Toward an Indigenous Theology of the Cross* (Philadelphia: Westminster, 1976); and Jürgen Moltmann, *The Crucified God: The Cross of Christ as the Foundation and Criticism*

of Christian Theology, trans. R. A. Wilson and John Bowden (London: SCM, 1974), among others.

13. We make no claims to being experts on postmodernism. Our reading of philosophers such as Derrida and Levinas has been shaped by reading Richard Kearney, especially *Strangers, Gods and Monsters: Interpreting Otherness* (London: Routledge, 2003), and *The God Who May Be: A Hermeneutics of Religion* (Bloomington: Indiana University Press, 2001).

14. The possibility that God may be a monster seems also to lie behind Luther's distinction between the hidden God and the revealed God in his treatise "Bondage of the Will." What this distinction does is to focus us on the God of promise who is revealed in the gospel and lead us away from speculations about the possible monstrosity of God.

15. We take the phrase "the possibility of the impossible" from Kearney. See, for example, Kearney, *Strangers*, 228.

16. The best book on distinguishing law and gospel remains C. F. W. Walther, *The Proper Distinction between Law and Gospel*, reproduced from the German edition of 1897, trans. W. H. T. Dau (St. Louis: Concordia, c. 1928). Obviously Walther addresses nineteenth-century issues with nineteenth-century concepts, but these can quite easily be translated into more contemporary issues and themes. For one attempt to do so, see Robert A. Kelly, "Preaching Good News in a Moralistic Age: Reflections on C. F. W. Walther's *Proper Distinction between Law and Gospel*," *Consensus* 31, no. 1 (2006): 47–71.

17. We are not advocating that law and gospel are to be used as a changeless structure for sermons, but as a tool for theological reflection and discernment. In this sense, what we are proposing is different from formulaic views of the gospel as a timeless kerygma or even homiletical views that posit a single, homiletical structure for all times and places. For a view of law and gospel as a constant homiletical structure, see the work of Paul Scott Wilson in *The Four Pages of the Sermon: A Guide to Biblical Preaching* (Nashville: Abingdon, 1999). Wilson finds similar examples of such law/gospel homiletical models in various works in recent homiletical theory in his book *Preaching and Homiletical Theory*, Preaching and Its Partners (St. Louis: Chalice, 2004), 73–100. For a critique of reified and dualistic views of law and gospel in light of Jewish/Christian relations, see David Schnasa Jacobsen and Günter Wasserberg, *Preaching Luke-Acts*, Preaching Classic Texts (Nashville: Abingdon, 2001), chap. 6.

18. The gospel might be heard embodied in human language or embodied in water and word. In either case it is a hearing of the word of God, a hearing of the gospel. It is also in either case a hearing of the gospel in community. When the gospel justifies by grace alone through faith alone, it justifies us as a community speaks the gospel to us and it initiates us into a community of the gospel.

19. The reader will no doubt be aware that we are basing our understanding of the interpretation of Scripture and tradition on the hermeneutics of Hans-Georg Gadamer and Paul Ricoeur. One can pursue this approach further in Hans-Georg Gadamer, *Truth and Method*, trans. Garret Barden and John Cumming (New York: Seabury, Continuum, 1975); idem, *Philosophical Hermeneutics*, ed. and trans. David E. Linge (Berkeley: University of California Press, 1977); and idem, "On the Circle of Understanding," in *Hermeneutics Versus Science? Three German Views, Essays by H.-G. Gadamer, E. K. Specht, W. Stegemüller*, ed. and trans. John M. Connolly and Thomas Keutner, Revisions: A Series of Books on Ethics, vol. 8 (Notre Dame, Ind.: University of Notre Dame Press, 1988). See also Paul Ricoeur, *The Conflict of Interpretation: Essays in Hermeneutics*, ed. Don Ihde, Northwestern University Studies in Phenomenology and Existential Philosophy (Evanston: Northwestern University Press, 1974); idem,

Time and Narrative, 2 vols., trans. Kathleen McLaughlin and David Pellauer (Chicago: University of Chicago Press, 1984–1985); and idem, *Essays on Biblical Interpretation*, intro. Lewis S. Mudge (Philadelphia: Fortress Press, 1980).

2. Gospel in Context and Situation

1. David Buttrick, *Homiletic: Moves and Structures* (Philadelphia: Fortress Press, 1987), 408–11.

2. The classic texts are Hans-Georg Gadamer, *Truth and Method*, trans. Garret Barden and John Cumming (New York: Seabury, 1975); and idem, *Philosophical Hermeneutics*, trans. David E. Linge (Berkeley: University of California Press, 1977); Paul Ricoeur, *The Conflict of Interpretation: Essays in Hermeneutics*, trans. Don Ihde (Evanston, Ill.: Northwestern University Press, 1974); idem, *The Rule of Metaphor: Multi-disciplinary Studies of the Creation of Meaning in Language*, trans. Robert Czerny, Kathleen McLaughlin, and John Costello (Toronto: University of Toronto Press, 1977); and idem, *Time and Narrative*, 3 vols., trans. Kathleen McLaughlin and David Pellauer (Chicago: University of Chicago Press, 1984–1988). We have also found Jürgen Habermas, *The Theory of Communicative Action*, 2 vols., trans. Thomas McCarthy (Boston: Beacon, 1984–1987), helpful.

3. Stephen B. Bevans, *Models of Contextual Theology*, rev. and exp. ed. (Maryknoll, N.Y.: Orbis, 2002), 37–140. The description below is based on Bevans's work.

4. A phrase from Douglas John Hall.

5. Ricoeur posits his "surplus of meaning" where a text is distanced from its producer through the act of writing, and thus its own "sense" from its original "reference." Thus, for Ricoeur this distanciation is not just problematic, but productive. See Paul Ricoeur, *Interpretation Theory: Discourse and the Surplus of Meaning* (Fort Worth: Texas Christian University Press, 1976), 44. Here we are applying Ricoeur's insight for a hermeneutic of texts to matters of situations and contexts.

6. The dialogue over the problems and possibilities of atonement theologies has been especially vigorous and fruitful of late. Preachers may want to read Marit Trelstad's edited volume *Cross Examinations: Readings on the Meaning of the Cross Today* (Minneapolis: Fortress Press, 2006) to get at the problematic, as well as to clarify differences between atonement theologies and the Lutheran theology of the cross generally. For attempts to reinvigorate a theology of the atonement with new metaphors, whether in theological writing or in sermons, see Mark D. Baker, ed., *Proclaiming the Scandal of the Cross: Contemporary Images of the Atonement* (Grand Rapids: Baker, 2006). The point is that culture need not be the enemy in theology. Though cultures can make hearing the gospel more difficult, cultures and cultural epochs can open new doors to theological understanding and an enlarged scope for matters of doctrine and practice.

7. About the tension of identity and relevance Jürgen Moltmann says, "These two crises are complementary. The more theology and the church attempt to become relevant to the problems of the present day, the more deeply they are drawn into the crisis of their own Christian identity. The more they attempt to assert their identity in traditional dogmas, rights and moral notions, the more irrelevant and unbelievable they become. This double crisis can be more accurately described as the *identity-involvement dilemma*." Moltmann, *The Crucified God: The Cross of Christ as the Foundation and Criticism of Christian Theology*, trans. R. A. Wilson and John Bowden (New York: Harper & Row, 1974), 7.

8. Jamie Swift, Jacqueline M. Davies, Robert G. Clarke, and Michael Czerny, S.J., *Getting Started on Social Analysis in Canada*, 4th ed., rev. and updated (Toronto: Between the Lines, 2003). The images and questions that follow come from *Getting Started*.

9. This phrase is from Ivan Illich, et al., *Disabling Professions* (London: M. Boyars, 1977).

10. We have both used the metaphor of the tree to describe social analysis so long that neither of us can remember where we learned it. We both know that we did not originate this metaphor; we learned it from others, but we cannot remember from whom. *Getting Started* points to four building blocks of the grammar of social analysis: symptoms, commodification, social costs, and structures (Swift, et al., *Getting Started,* 72ff.)

11. Ibid., 525.

12. Edward Farley, "Interpreting Situations: An Inquiry into the Nature of Practical Theology," in *Formation and Reflection: The Promise of Practical Theology,* ed. Lewis Mudge and James Poling (Philadelphia: Fortress Press, 1987), 1–26.

13. Ibid., 11–14. Our description that follows is a synopsis of Farley's arguments in this part of his article.

14. Ibid., 14.

3. Preaching Gospel at Funerals

1. One such corporation is Service Corporation International (SCI), which almost always retains the traditional name of funeral homes and cemeteries it has purchased so it is not obvious to people that the concern is owned by a large multinational corporation. SCI was formed in 2006 in a merger of two previous giants, Service Corporation of Houston and Alderwoods. In 1999 Service had formed the Dignity Memorial "brand" and most SCI funeral homes and cemeteries in the United States and Canada operate as part of Dignity Memorial. In the town where we live, half of the funeral homes are owned by Dignity Memorial, though, as is common in the industry, all operate under their historic names. For more information on the major corporations, see the Funeral Consumers Alliance at http://www.funerals.org/; for Ontario, Canada, the equivalent is http://www.myfuneralplan.org/ (both accessed March 31, 2009).

2. Jessica Mitford, *The American Way of Death Revisited* (New York: Knopf, 1998), a revision of *The American Way of Death* (New York: Simon & Schuster, 1963, rev. 1978).

3. Stanley French, "The Cemetery as Cultural Institution: The Establishment of Mount Auburn and the 'Rural Cemetery' Movement," in *Death in America,* ed., with intro. by David E. Stannard (Philadelphia: University of Pennsylvania Press, 1975), 69–91.

4. For Tyler Cassity's latest innovation in cemeteries, see Tad Friend, "The Shroud of Marin: Tyler Cassity and the New Way of Death," *The New Yorker,* August 29, 2005, 50–63.

5. Ibid., 52.

6. Ronald G. E. Smith, *The Death Care Industries in the United States* (Jefferson, N.C.: McFarland & Co., 1996), 343–44.

7. Mitford, *American Way,* 145–49.

8. Some of the works we and our colleagues have found most helpful are:

Billman, Kathleen D., and Daniel L. Migliori. *Rachel's Cry: Prayer of Lament and Rebirth of Hope.* Cleveland: United Church Press, 1999.

Doka, Kenneth J., ed. *Living with Grief after Sudden Loss: Suicide, Homicide, Accident, Heart Attack, Stroke.* Washington, D.C.: Hospice Foundation of America/Bristol, Pa.: Taylor & Francis, 1996.

Grollman, Earl A., ed. *Explaining Death to Children.* Boston: Beacon, 1967.

Lewis, C. S. *A Grief Observed.* London: Faber and Faber, 1961.

Nouwen, Henri J. M. *A Letter of Consolation.* San Francisco: Harper & Row, 1982.

Rosen, Helen. *Unspoken Grief: Coping with Childhood Sibling Loss.* Lexington, Mass.; Toronto: D. C. Heath, 1986.

9. John McKnight, *The Careless Society: Community and Its Counterfeits* (New York: Basic Books, 1995), 3–4.

10. Ibid., 6.

11. This is a term for the church from Douglas John Hall.

12. This phrase is Latin for "simultaneously just and sinful," which is often stated as "saint and sinner." It is an essential part of Lutheran anthropology, which claims that the justified person is equally and simultaneously a child of Adam and Eve who therefore continues to suffer the results of the fall and a child of Christ who is justified and sanctified by grace through faith.

13. Martin Luther, "Psalm 90," in *Selected Psalms II, Luther's Works* (American Edition), vol. 13, trans. Paul M. Bretscher, ed. Jaroslav Pelikan (St. Louis: Concordia, 1956), 73–141.

4. Preaching Gospel at Weddings

1. http://elcic.ca/Same-Sex-Blessings/Essays.cfm (accessed February 25, 2009).

2. The classic interpretation of Luther's views on marriage is William Lazareth, *Luther on the Christian Home: An Application of the Social Ethics of the Reformation* (Philadelphia: Muhlenberg, 1960). For a more current interpretation, see Scott Hendrix, "Luther on Marriage," in Timothy J. Wengert, ed., *Harvesting Martin Luther's Reflections on Theology, Ethics, and the Church,* Lutheran Quarterly Books (Grand Rapids: Eerdmans, 2004), 169–84.

3. Charles Taylor, *Sources of the Self: The Making of the Modern Identity* (Cambridge: Harvard University Press, 1989).

4. Ibid., 211.

5. Ibid., 213.

6. Ibid., 217–18.

7. See, e.g., *Luther's Works,* vol. 54, *Table Talk,* ed. Theodore G. Tappert (Philadelphia: Fortress Press, 1967), 363–64 (No. 4716).

8. Stanley Hauerwas, *After Christendom: How the Church Is to Behave If Freedom, Justice, and a Christian Nation Are Bad Ideas* (Nashville: Abingdon, 1991), 127.

9. For good examples, see Peter Brown, *The Body and Society: Men, Women, and Sexual Renunciation in Early Christianity,* Lectures on the History of Religions, vol. 13 (New York: Columbia University Press, 1988); and R. A. Markus, *The End of Ancient Christianity* (Cambridge: Cambridge University Press, 1990).

10. See, among others, Stanley Hauerwas, *A Community of Character: Toward a Constructive Christian Social Ethic* (Notre Dame, Ind.: University of Notre Dame Press, 1981), 155–74; idem, *After Christendom,* 113–31; and idem, *A Better Hope: Resources for a Church Confronting Capitalism, Democracy, and Postmodernity* (Grand Rapids: Brazos, 2000), 47–51.

11. See Thomas de Zengotita, *Mediated: How the Media Shapes Your World and the Way You Live in It* (New York: Bloomsbury, 2005). Also good in regard to the place of the nonconsumer in the present world is Zygmunt Bauman, *Work, Consumerism, and the New Poor,* Issues in Society (Philadelphia: Open University Press, 1998).

12. A phrase for the church borrowed from Douglas John Hall.

13. One might argue that the controversy around polygamy among Christians in parts of Africa is a counterexample. It is possible, though, that this is an example of a tension between European/North American culture brought by missionaries and indigenous cultures more than a conflict between "Christian" views of marriage and "pagan" views of marriage.

14. We have found Colin Gunton, *The Triune Creator: A Historical and Systematic Study* (Grand Rapids: Eerdmans, 1998), to be helpful in thinking about the doctrine of creation. See also Jürgen Moltmann, *God in Creation: An Ecological Doctrine of Creation*, The Gifford Lectures, 1984–1985, trans. Margaret Kohl (London: SCM, 1985).

15. Obviously, the "for others" represents Dietrich Bonhoeffer's influence on us. We are also influenced by the thought of Douglas John Hall as he presents it in *The Steward: A Biblical Symbol Come of Age*, rev. ed. (Grand Rapids: Eerdmans, 1990). See also chap. 5 below on stewardship preaching.

16. For a survey of and original contribution to the conversation on otherness, see Richard Kearney, *Strangers, Gods and Monsters: Interpreting Otherness* (London: Routledge, 2003).

17. *Lutheran Book of Worship* (Minneapolis: Augsburg/Philadelphia: Board of Publication, Lutheran Church in America, 1978), 203.

18. This point is made by Jürgen Moltmann, *The Crucified God: The Cross of Christ as the Foundation and Criticism of Christian Theology*, trans. R. A. Wilson and John Bowden (London: SCM, 1974).

5. Preaching Gospel and Stewardship

1. Some of the classic studies of "success literature" are Richard M. Huber, *The American Idea of Success* (New York: McGraw-Hill, 1971); Moses Rischin, ed., *The American Gospel of Success: Individualism and Beyond* (Chicago: Quadrangle, 1965); Richard Weiss, *The American Myth of Success: From Horatio Alger to Norman Vincent Peale* (New York: Basic Books, 1969); and Irvin G. Wyllie, *The Self-Made Man in America: The Myth of Rags to Riches* (New York: Free Press, 1954). In Bob's research he has found that the differences between examples of American and Canadian success literature are subtle because both grow from the root of English and Scottish Calvinism. Cf. Robert A. Kelly, "The Gospel of Success in Canada: Charles W. Gordon (Ralph Connor) as Exemplar," *Historical Papers 1998*, Canadian Society of Church History, Annual Conference, University of Ottawa, 29–30 May 1998, ed. Bruce L. Guenther (n.p.: Canadian Society of Church History, 1998), 5–15; and Robert A. Kelly, "Successful or Justified? The North American Doctrine of Salvation by Works," *Concordia Theological Quarterly* 65, no. 3 (July 2001): 224–45. The typology of success literature as "character," "mind power," and "winning personality" is from Huber.

2. Thomas Frank, *The Conquest of Cool: Business Culture, Counterculture, and the Rise of Hip Consumerism* (Chicago: University of Chicago Press, 1997).

3. This is not to say that middle-class people in North America do not work hard and long, but that their reasons for working long and hard are not what they used to be.

4. Thomas de Zengotita, *Mediated: How the Media Shapes Your World and the Way You Live in It* (New York: Bloomsbury, 2005).

5. Robert D. Putnam, *Bowling Alone: The Collapse and Revival of American Community* (New York: Simon & Schuster, 2000).

6. John de Graff, David Wann, and Thomas H. Naylor, *Affluenza: The All-Consuming Epidemic,* 2d ed. (San Francisco: Berrett-Koehler, 2005).

7. All quotes are from the Iona Community Web site: http://www.iona.org.uk/ (accessed February 25, 2009).

8. The complete discipline is: "Daily prayer and reading the Bible; Mutual sharing and accountability for our use of time and money; Regular meeting together; and Action and reflection for justice, peace and the integrity of creation." http://www.iona.org.uk/iona_community.php (accessed February 25, 2009).

9. *Luther's Works*, vol. 35, *Word and Sacrament I*, ed. E. Theodore Bachman, Helmut T. Lehmann, gen. ed. (Philadelphia: Fortress Press, 1960), 52.

10. This was brought to the attention of many through Robert N. Bellah, et al., *Habits of the Heart: Individualism and Commitment in American Life* (Berkeley: University of California Press, 1985). For a recent example of research, see David Kinnaman and Gabe Lyons, *unChristian: What a New Generation Really Thinks about Christianity . . . and Why It Matters* (Grand Rapids: Baker, 2007).

11. See Greg Hawkins and Cally Parkinson, *Reveal: Where Are You?* (Chicago: Willow Creek Association, 2007).

6. Preaching Gospel in the Face of Injustice

1. Homiletician Paul Scott Wilson argues that conservative and liberal preaching alike are plagued by moralism (*Four Pages of the Sermon: A Guide to Biblical Preaching* [Nashville: Abingdon, 1999], 20–21). While we agree that gospel preaching is something other than mere ethical browbeating, we would also like to argue that the gospel in this context can have a more pronounced social and political content. Attention to the context surrounding situations where we articulate the gospel in the face of injustice means that the gospel is not merely "joyful" theocentric news about what God "does," but specifically news about what God does to "liberate" and free us for our neighbors.

2. Farley's concern with moralism here is accompanied by a concern for two other cultural trends: bureaucracy and therapy—all of which can provide models for church leadership at the expense of the theological task. Edward Farley, *Practicing Gospel: Unconventional Thoughts on the Church's Ministry* (Louisville: Westminster John Knox, 2003), 9.

3. Henry H. Mitchell, *Celebration and Experience in Preaching* (Nashville: Abingdon, 1990), 63.

4. Walter Brueggemann summarizes the value of this distinction for prophetic preaching and a prophetic ministry generally in *The Prophetic Imagination* (Philadelphia: Fortress Press, 1978), 111.

5. See Gerhard Ebeling's article "The Necessity of the Doctrine of the Two Kingdoms" in his book *Word and Faith*, trans. J. Leitch (Philadelphia: Fortress Press, 1963), 386–406.

6. Robert N. Bellah, et al., *Habits of the Heart: Individualism and Commitment in American Life* (Berkeley: University of California Press, 1985).

7. Parker Palmer, *The Company of Strangers: Christians and the Renewal of America's Public Life* (New York: Crossroad, 1985).

8. The "invisible hand" is a reference to Adam Smith's almost theological metaphor for talking about the ways in which free markets work in his book *The Wealth of Nations*. In a world where the divide between rich and poor is growing, savvy preachers should be worried about such mystifying theological metaphors as wielded by economists!

9. David Buttrick, *Homiletic: Moves and Structures* (Philadelphia: Fortress Press, 1987), 277–78.

10. The phrase in Latin, of course, is in the singular. Our presupposition, however, is that ecclesial awareness is a shared, social, theological reality.

11. Martin Luther, "The Freedom of a Christian," in *Career of the Reformer: I*, vol. 31, *Luther's Works*, trans. W. A. Lambert, rev. and ed. H. Grimm (Philadelphia: Muhlenberg, 1957), 364–71.

12. John Hope Franklin, *From Slavery to Freedom*, 3d ed. (New York: Knopf, 1967 [1947]), 282ff.

13. Ibid., 285–86.

14. David has treated this issue in greater detail in his article, "*Schola Prophetarum*: Prophetic Preaching toward a Public, Prophetic Church," in *Homiletic* 34:1 (2009), 12–21.

15. In Lutheran theology this kind of argument reflects the distinction between the revealed God (*Deus revelatus*) and the hidden God (*Deus absconditus*). Theologically, the principle is that we start from the God we know, the One disclosed in the life, ministry, death, and resurrection of Jesus Christ. For more on this distinction, see Robert Kolb's *Bound Choice, Election, and Wittenberg Theological Method* (Grand Rapids: Eerdmans, 2005), 35–38.

16. The argument here is in part inspired by the work of René Girard, *I See Satan Fall Like Lightning,* trans. J. Williams (Maryknoll, N.Y.: Orbis, 2001). Girard views Jesus' death as the conclusion of a series of revelations—which begin with the Hebrew Scriptures—of our very human "single victim mechanism." This revelation exposes the cycle of mimetic violence and the exoneration of the community that the mechanism entails (social self-justification?). In fact, in the cross God takes the side of the innocent, scapegoated victim as the means of showing that cycle for what it really is.

17. The quote refers to the title of Douglas John Hall's own work on the theology of the cross, *Lighten Our Darkness: Towards an Indigenous Theology of the Cross* (Philadelphia: Westminster, 1976).

18. For more on this critique of prophetic preaching, see David's article, "*Schola Prophetarum*: Prophetic Preaching toward a Public, Prophetic Church" (see n. 14, above).

7. Preaching Gospel in Times of Public Crises

1. Edward Farley, *Practicing Gospel: Unconventional Thoughts on the Church's Ministry* (Louisville: Westminster John Knox, 2003), 9. In this chapter, Farley identifies three potential "reductions": the bureaucratic mind-set (which we identified with management), the individualistic paradigm (which we call therapy), and the moralistic. While the pervasive power of our culture's concern for moralism is problematic for the gospel preacher, our treatment of the gospel in the terms laid out in chap. 2 should have already disabused the reader of that cultural paradigm in the pulpit!

2. Those familiar with the literature of homiletics will recognize the influence of David Buttrick and Ron Allen on this point. For Buttrick's view of such issues and his "preaching in the mode of praxis," see *Homiletic: Moves and Structures* (Philadelphia: Fortress Press, 1987), 405–45. For Allen, see his books *Preaching the Topical Sermon* (Louisville: Westminster John Knox, 1991), 5ff., and *Preaching the Gospel* (St. Louis: Chalice, 1999), 65–85. For why the public square might be important for the preaching task, see also John McClure's *The Roundtable Pulpit: Where Leadership and Preaching Meet* (Nashville: Abingdon, 1995), 18–19.

3. Neil Postman, *Amusing Ourselves to Death: Public Discourse in the Age of Show Business* (New York: Penguin, 1985). What follows are three key elements of Postman's much more extensive analysis.

4. Ibid., 86ff.

5. Ibid., 99–113.

6. The idea that media might also "form" the shape of human awareness is not a new one. Walter Ong argues that the human "*sensorium*" is shaped by the dominant media of a given cultural epoch in *The Presence of the Word: Some Prolegomena for Cultural and Religious History* (New Haven: Yale University Press, 1967), 1–16.

7. Postman, *Amusing Ourselves*, 87.

8. Ibid., 87–88.

9. Katherine Hall Jamieson, *Eloquence in an Electronic Age: The Transformation of Political Speechmaking* (New York: Oxford University Press, 1988).

10. Roger Ailes, *You Are the Message: Getting What You Want by Being Who You Are* (New York: Currency, 1988).

11. Preachers in a political context like ours should always be mindful of the will-to-power that lurks in a pulpited self-disclosure in our culture. Perhaps Paul's words might not sound quite so odd to our itching ears in our better moments: "For we do not proclaim ourselves; we proclaim Jesus Christ as Lord and ourselves as your slaves for Jesus' sake (2 Cor. 4:5). Homiletician André Resner has made a spirited case for an appropriate kind of pulpit self-disclosure in his book *Preacher and Cross: Person and Message in Theology and Rhetoric* (Grand Rapids: Eerdmans, 1999). However, so far as we know, such advocates for even a modified homiletical self-disclosure have never dealt with the problem posed by the broader cultural and political issues we are raising here.

12. Edward S. Herman and Noam Chomsky, *Manufacturing Consent* (New York: Pantheon, 1988), 32.

13. Ibid., 33.

14. Ibid., 35.

15. With the aid of our colleagues in other practical-theological disciplines, we have assembled a brief bibliography to help pastors use such skills wisely:

Pastoral Care

Billman, Kathleen, and Daniel L. Migliore. *Rachel's Cry: Prayer of Lament and Rebirth of Hope*. Cleveland: United Church Press, 1999.

Meier, Augustine, Thomas St. James O'Connor, and Peter van Katwyk. *Spirituality and Health: Multi-Disciplinary Explorations*. Waterloo, Ont.: Wilfrid Laurier University Press, 2005.

Patton, John. *Pastoral Care in Context*. Louisville: Westminster John Knox, 1993.

Poling, James Newton. *Render unto God: Economic Violence and Pastoral Theology*. St. Louis: Chalice, 2002.

Leadership

Friedman, Edwin H. *From Generation to Generation: Family Process in Church and Synagogue*. New York: Guilford, 1985.

Steinke, Peter. *Healthy Congregations*. Bethesda, Md.: Alban Institute, 1996.

16. Martha Simmons and Frank A. Thomas, eds., 9.11.01: *African American Leaders Respond to an American Tragedy* (Valley Forge, Pa.: Judson, 2001), x.

17. We were unable to locate the exact source of this phrase.

18. For more on this interpretation of this narrative from Luke's Gospel, see David Schnasa Jacobsen and Günter Wasserberg, *Preaching Luke-Acts* (Nashville: Abingdon, 2001), 19–35.

19. Wendy Farley, *Tragic Vision and Divine Compassion: A Contemporary Theodicy* (Louisville: Westminster John Knox, 1990).

20. Ibid., 132.

21. While there are elements of human freedom and accountability within tragedies, there is an important, sometimes even controlling, role for the "fates" as well. Aristotle in his *Poetics* argues that the beauty of the tragic plot is in its movement of "necessity." We are not sure that Farley isn't actually trading one form of arbitrary determinism that emphasizes divine sovereignty for another. We are also still unsure what "redemption" means here. Although she is quick to reject such language early on, she returns to the category to describe the work of divine compassion in radical suffering. It strikes us that the way she uses it stretches the term beyond recognition. Along the way she also takes a swipe at eschatological language, as if all of it encour-

aged acquiescence to evil in the face of the sweet by-and-by. Although it is true that some eschatological language functions in that way, eschatological language is valuable precisely in sustaining a life of resistance to evil and radical suffering. "Keep your eyes on the prize," "We shall overcome," and many other civil rights slogans use the language of eschatology not to escape, but to engage evil more deeply and directly.

22. As quoted by Carmine DiSante in his book *Jewish Prayer: The Origins of Christian Liturgy* (New York: Paulist, 1985), 168.

23. Ibid.

24. The language of the cross as a key signature for theology comes from Douglas John Hall, *The Cross in Our Context: Jesus and the Suffering World* (Minneapolis: Fortress Press, 2003).

X. Preaching Gospel Going Forward

1. The latter is a point made quite ably by several people in contemporary homiletics. Ron Allen has surfaced this issue in several books, most recently in his fine book *Preaching Is Believing: The Sermon as Theological Reflection* (Louisville: Westminster John Knox, 2002), esp. 37–62. In several writings Allen has called his understanding of the gospel "the dipolar news of God's unconditional love for each and all and God's will for justice for each and all" (ibid., 17). Our colleague at the Toronto School of Theology, Paul Scott Wilson, in his text *The Four Pages of the Sermon* (Nashville: Abingdon, 1999), argues that the gospel is best represented through a basic deep structure that names law in the text as equivalent to law in our world and relating these to a proclamation of gospel or grace in the text as equivalent to the same in our world. More recently he has nuanced his position in his article, "Preach the Text or Preach the Gospel?" in the e-journal *TST Homiletics Seminar* 1, no. 1 (Winter 2007): 1–10, which can be found archived at http://individual.utoronto.ca/jacobsen1/TSTHS1-1.pdf for personal reading (accessed March 2, 2009). We believe that every preacher has at least an implicit view of what the gospel is. Sometimes homileticians do not spell out consistently what their view of the gospel is, especially when not writing an explicit theology of preaching. For a tool of interpreting an implicit or explicit theology of the gospel by reading someone's homiletical *theory*, see chap. 1 of L. Susan Bond's fine book *Contemporary African American Preaching: Diversity in Theory and Style* (St. Louis: Chalice, 2003), esp. 5–8.

2. Preachers may wish to read Robert McAfee Brown's *Saying Yes and Saying No: On Rendering to God and Caesar* (Philadelphia: Westminster, 1986).

3. The classic treatment of this issue is theologian Douglas John Hall's *Has the Church a Future?* (Philadelphia: Fortress Press, 1980).

4. A classic treatment of this problem is found in Stanley Hauerwas and William Willimon's *Resident Aliens: Life in the Christian Colony* (Nashville: Abingdon, 1989).

5. No doubt, private school baccalaureates would be an altogether different event viewed contextually. For purposes of our situation, however, we are viewing this situation as happening in a public school context.

6. We saw something similar in our chapter on preaching gospel at weddings. Marriage is not something that needs to be redeemed or sanctified. It is part of God's good order of creation and is addressed as such homiletically.

7. Please see the appendix for preachers below for more detailed suggestions about how to use gospel commonplaces in your preaching.

Appendix for Preachers

1. This does not mean, of course, that Scripture is not already part of our gospel reflections. Many of the gospel commonplaces in the previous chapters refer-

ence Scripture. The distinction is a subtle one. Theologian Edward Farley, in his book on theological method, *Ecclesial Reflection: An Anatomy of Theological Method* (Philadelphia: Fortress Press, 1982), 272–81, argues that Scripture functions not on the a priori authoritative basis of the so-called Scripture *principle*, but within theological reflection as part of a linguistic sedimentation of kerygma in relation to the tradition. Even when we preach from a biblical text, the underlying theological purpose of preaching still holds true: the text exists to help us preach the gospel. If, however, one were fortunate to be in a situation that called for sustained theological reflection on a biblical theme, one might also try to approach the situational gospel sermon thematically through several texts. For a careful *theological* way through such a thematic approach, see Ron Allen, *Wholly Scripture: Preaching Biblical Themes* (St. Louis: Chalice, 2004).

2. Some helpful texts that contain some suggestions for using a gospel commonplace this way might be found in some of the following recent works in homiletics: Ronald Allen, *Preaching the Topical Sermon* (Louisville: Westminster John Knox, 1992), 75–77, 84–86; and Jane Rzepka and Ken Sawyer, *Thematic Preaching: An Introduction* (St. Louis: Chalice, 2001).

3. Allen, *Preaching the Topical Sermon*, 11–14.

4. The whole notion of preaching inductively received its most well-known articulation in the seminal work of homiletician Fred Craddock. For the latest edition of his work, see *As One without Authority*, rev. ed. (St. Louis: Chalice, 2001).

5. Notice as we think about either of these two approaches to using a gospel commonplace, we are also using the situation and context to think about the appropriateness of the deductive or inductive models at a given moment. Context affects not only what we say in a gospel commonplace, but how we say it in thinking through matters of sermon form. For more insightful reflection on this question, see Fred Craddock, *Preaching* (Nashville: Abingdon, 1985), 180–82.

6. An analysis of this particular text by C. H. Dodd in his *The Apostolic Preaching and Its Development* (London: Hodder and Stoughton, 1936), esp. 21–24, is a key part of his argument for a "core" to the gospel in an early Christian kerygma. Unlike Dodd, we argue for a more fluid sense of the gospel that is not simply reducible to the facts about Jesus set within an eschatological framework. While cross and resurrection are central to a gospel focused on the radical grace of God, the gospel ought not be reduced to any fixed, timeless kerygmatic rehearsal.

7. The language of a structural "theo-logic" harks back to the work of David Buttrick in *Homiletic: Moves and Structures* (Philadelphia: Fortress Press, 1987).

8. Craddock, *As One*, 122–23.

9. Buttrick, *Homiletic*, 70–75. For a more detailed treatment of how situational preaching impacts issues of sermon structure, see Buttrick, 427–45.

10. Edward Farley, *Practicing Gospel: Unconventional Thoughts on the Church's Ministry* (Louisville: Westminster John Knox, 2003), 80.

11. Ibid.

12. For ways in which preaching a biblical text might prompt similar reflections about the relationship between gospel and world, see David Schnasa Jacobsen, *Preaching in the New Creation: The Promise of New Testament Apocalyptic Texts* (Louisville: Westminster John Knox, 1999).

ANNOTATED BIBLIOGRAPHY FOR GOSPEL-PREACHING RESIDENTIAL THEOLOGIANS

Theologies of the Gospel

Farley, Edward. *Practicing Gospel: Unconventional Thoughts on the Church's Ministry*. Louisville: Westminster John Knox, 2003. Part 2 of this work reflects on what the gospel is and how it is important for a pulpit that tends to focus more on preaching texts than preaching gospel.

Forde, Gerhard O. *Theology Is for Proclamation*. Minneapolis: Fortress Press, 1990. Offers a neoorthodox Lutheran view of the gospel and relates it to the preaching task.

Pittenger, Norman W. *Preaching the Gospel*. London: Morehouse, 1984. Pittenger develops his theology of the gospel from a process perspective.

Theological Method

Allen, Ronald J. *Preaching Is Believing: The Sermon as Theological Reflection*. Louisville: Westminster John Knox, 2002. This book is wonderful for relating all of preaching to systematic theology and reflecting on the way in which theology's sources and norms shape the homiletical task.

Campbell, Charles L. *The Word before the Powers: An Ethic of Preaching*. Louisville: Westminster John Knox, 2002. Campbell offers an important postliberal approach to thinking about the relationship of preaching to a character-based theological ethic. It would be an example of a homiletical-theological method that applies the strange word of the Scriptures to life lived "before the powers."

Cooper, Burton Z., and John S. McClure. *Claiming Theology in the Pulpit*. Louisville: Westminster John Knox, 2003. Helps preachers discern their own theological profile and use it as a tool for thinking theologically through sermons.

Kolb, Robert. *Bound Choice, Election, and Wittenberg Theological Method*. Grand Rapids: Eerdmans, 2005. Helps readers understand Reformation Lutheran theological method through the lens of Luther's "Bondage of the Will" and the historical development of doctrine to the Formula of Concord.

Wells, Harold. *The Christic Center: Life-Giving and Liberating*. Maryknoll, N.Y.: Orbis, 2004. Argues for a christological center as a focus for a contextualized theological method.

Contextualizing the Gospel

Bellah, Robert N., et al. *Habits of the Heart: Individualism and Commitment in American Life*. New York: Harper & Row, 1985. This book is most useful for pastors who struggle to think about the gospel beyond the terms of therapeutic individualism, which has been a particularly thorny problem for the North American pulpit.

Bevans Stephen B. *Models of Contextual Theology.* Rev. and exp. ed. Maryknoll, N.Y.: Orbis, 2002. Lays out a variety of options for thinking about the relationship of gospel to culture and context. This is a must-read for a residential theologian.

Hall, Douglas John. *The Cross in Our Context: Jesus and the Suffering World.* Minneapolis: Fortress Press, 2003. Hall attempts to develop a contextual North American theology that takes seriously a theology of the cross.

Hopewell, James F. *Congregation: Stories and Structures.* Ed. Barbara Wheeler. Philadelphia: Fortress Press, 1987. Hopewell's book tries to get an appreciation for congregations' ways of storying their own lives using literary critic Northrop Frye's four narrative genres: the comic, the romantic, the tragic, and the ironic. Hopewell's insights about congregations can be fruitfully used in thinking about relating gospel to context.

Nieman, James R. *Knowing the Context: Frames, Tools, and Structures for Preaching.* Elements of Preaching. Minneapolis: Fortress Press, 2008. Nieman brings the discussion of preaching and context to a new level. Although the focus remains on the more interpersonal elements of context, the book is very helpful for discerning the pastoral task of contextual preaching.

Smith, Christine M. *Preaching as Weeping, Confession, and Resistance: Radical Reponses to Radical Evil.* Louisville: Westminster John Knox, 1992. Does a great job of relating preaching to contextual moments of radical evil. In doing so, Smith relates theology to proclamation.

Solberg, Mary. M. *Compelling Knowledge: A Feminist Proposal for an Epistemology of the Cross.* Albany: State University of New York Press, 1997. Solberg, having experienced a theology of suffering in El Salvador, turns to her own North American context to make sense of the cross using the categories of epistemology.

Tisdale, Leonora Tubbs. *Preaching as Local Theology and Folk Art.* Fortress Resources for Preaching. Minneapolis: Fortress Press, 1997. Offers direction for using the tools of the ethnographer for getting at the operative "local theology" of a congregation.

Gospel and Situations

Farley, Edward. "Interpreting Situations: An Inquiry into the Nature of Practical Theology." In *Practicing Gospel: Unconventional Thoughts on the Church's Ministry,* 29–43. Louisville: Westminster John Knox, 2003. (Originally appeared as an essay in L. Mudge and J. Poling, eds., *Formation and Reflection* [Philadelphia: Fortress Press, 1987].) Considers the many dimensions of situations and invites readers to consider their interpretation as central to the task of practical theology.

Situational Preaching

Aden, LeRoy H., and Robert G. Hughes. *Preaching God's Compassion.* Fortress Resources for Preaching. Minneapolis: Fortress Press, 2002. Aden and Hughes relate specific situations for preaching to the resources of pastoral theology. While their pastoral concerns are not as broad as the contextual/situational ones we highlight, in moments of personal and interpersonal care, their homiletical reflections can be quite helpful.

Allen, Ronald J. *Preaching the Topical Sermon.* Louisville: Westminster John Knox, 1992. A wonderful basic book on the broader category of topical preaching, whose concerns also include the sort of situational preaching and focus on the gospel we treat in the preceding pages here.

Buttrick, David G. *Homiletic: Moves and Structures*. Philadelphia: Fortress Press, 1987. The section on "preaching in the mode of praxis" toward the end of Buttrick's book articulates a useful way for thinking about situational preaching that is both theological and rhetorical.

Jacobsen, David Schnasa. "Proclaiming the Gospel in Situations: Theological Commonplaces for Occasions in Ministry and Life." *TST Homiletics Seminar* 1, no. 1 (Winter 2007): 15–18. http://individual.utoronto.ca/jacobsen1/TSTHS1-1.pdf (accessed March 2, 2009). In this e-journal article the author makes a brief case for the kind of homiletical-theological reflection necessary for doing situational preaching using gospel "commonplaces."

———, with Robert Kelly. "Preaching the Wedding Sermon: Toward a Theology of Marriage for the Pulpit." *Clergy Journal* 74, no. 5 (March, 2008): 43–44. In this article the authors articulate four theological principles for thinking about wedding sermons in light of a context that struggles over the secularity and holiness of marriage. The authors argue for a gospel preaching that focuses on the ordinariness of marriage in creation.

Schlafer, David J. *What Makes This Day Different: Preaching Grace on Special Occasions*. Cambridge, Mass.: Cowley, 1998. Schlafer's book is helpful in that it relates grace to occasions in church life. While he does not develop the full resources of systematic theology from which we attempt to draw, Schlafer's book can be useful for thinking especially about recurring occasions in church life and public calendars.

Simmons, Martha, and Frank A. Thomas, eds. *9.11.01: African American Leaders Respond to an American Tragedy*. Valley Forge, Pa.: Judson, 2001. In this book preachers will find some sustained theological work on a specific crisis. The work includes many helpful sermons.

INDEX